Trustful Surrender

Debbie Georgianni and Jerry Usher

Trustful Surrender

Stories of Grace Amidst Crisis

EWTN PUBLISHING, INC.
Irondale, Alabama

EWTN Publishing, Inc.
5817 Old Leeds Road, Irondale, AL 35210

Distributed by Sophia Institute Press, Box 5284, Manchester, NH 03108.

paperback ISBN 978-168278-126-5

ebook ISBN 978-1-68278-127-2

Library of Congress Control Number: 2020933219

First printing

*To the "Take 2 Family": without you,
this book would not be possible.*

*And to the "Powerhouse Six,"
to whom we pray before every show:
Our Lady of Fatima, St. Joseph,
St. Michael the Archangel, St. Teresa of Calcutta,
St. Padre Pio, and Mother Angelica.*

Contents

Foreword

"I don't know what happened. We sent our kids to Catholic school. They got confirmed. They went to Mass with us every Sunday. We sent them to college, and now they're telling us they no longer believe anything the Church teaches."

"My fiancé, who is Lutheran, was open to being married in the Catholic Church. We went to a priest, who discouraged us, so I left the Catholic Faith and got married in my fiancé's church."

"Why would a loving God allow me to have been abused for so long? There must not be a God, and if there is, He doesn't love me."

There are many reasons why people leave the Church. Above are just a few examples from people I have encountered at conferences or parish missions over the years. There is a common thread woven through these experiences: the collateral damage to those who remain in the Church. Estranged parents, grandparents, siblings, and friends must bear painful and often overwhelming feelings of abandonment and isolation. Conversations and encounters that were once loving and filled with laughter are now relentlessly argumentative and utterly frustrating — if they occur at all.

We all know that serious issues are often not addressed in families. None of us wants to acknowledge the resentment and pain that have built up for years; instead, we just go about our lives pretending everything is fine. Yet the gospel calls each of us to repent and convert; to surrender ourselves completely in love and trust to Our Lord and Savior Jesus Christ, and not to the opinions of the world.

EWTN's popular radio show *Take 2 with Jerry and Debbie* has been a blessing in the lives of so many listeners. Jerry and Debbie have created a format for the faithful to share the joy of reaching new levels of holiness, the heartache of life's many challenges, and the exhilaration of victory over the power of sin. All this occurs within a supportive, grace-filled setting that fosters intimacy with the Lord.

This book contains stories from listeners whose loved ones have left the Catholic Church. Together, these stories serve as a source of hope. They help us to see that, as the Body of Christ, we must not be afraid to follow Jesus, nor to live truly our baptismal call to holiness, wherever we are on our journey through life. We must allow the floodwaters of Baptism to destroy the selfishness, egotism, and sinfulness that prevent us from becoming sons and daughters of the truth, as God intended.

This is critical precisely because today's culture presents the Church with many difficulties as Her faithful struggle to live the gospel. We so easily let the king of lies into our hearts when we are angry with someone we love; when we struggle with depression, addiction, or abuse; and when we are tempted to do what feels good at the expense of our dignity and self-worth. In these experiences, we must stand at the foot of the Cross with deep compassion and unwavering fervor, while always speaking the truth in love to those who have left the Church and no longer practice the Faith.

Foreword

Trustful Surrender is a beautiful reminder that we are all called to be saints. Saints are people who have responded generously to the love of God. They have survived the pains and challenges of this world; they have lived the Beatitudes; they have washed their robes white in the Blood of the Lamb; and they now rejoice and share in the total victory of Christ. Allow the faith journeys in the pages that follow to draw you into a place where there is nothing standing between you and your ability to become the saint God created you to be. Let us pray for all those who have left the Church that they may finally give themselves over to God's will, preferring absolutely nothing to the love of Christ.

—Deacon Harold Burke-Sivers, M.T.S.
Author, *Father Augustus Tolton: The Slave Who Became the First African-American Priest*
January 12, 2020
Feast of the Baptism of the Lord

Introduction

Trustful Surrender is the fruit of decades of ministry on the part of Jerry Usher and Debbie Georgianni. The number-one prayer intention they've heard as they've traveled the world promoting the Catholic Faith is for loved ones who left the Faith. The fact that this is as important as it is to people is a sign of how seriously they take their Catholic Faith. But it's also a source of tremendous heartache and pain. The people in this book have known that pain. Some are still in the midst of it. As you'll see when you read these pages, some of the authors have known the incredible joy of seeing their loved ones return to the sacraments. Others are still awaiting that tremendous gift. A few even saw their loved ones enter eternity before enjoying any visible sign of their return to the fold. The most important lesson for every reader is that God is always reaching out to His children. He never gives up on us. Let's never give up on Him, especially His grace leading our loved ones home.

"Daddy, Where Are You Going to Put the Grass?"

By Joseph Harrison

∞

"Daddy, where are you going to put the grass?"

I asked my dad this question after he had finished erecting a swing set in our basement. At such a young age, I hadn't yet realized that grass couldn't grow out of a concrete floor. Like most small children, I saw my dad as someone who could do anything, even make grass grow indoors. There was only one thing he couldn't do for me and my four siblings: make his marriage to my mom last.

For as long as I can remember, there had been strife in our home. Mom was very, well, mothering to all of us, including Dad. She was emotionally needy. As I can see by looking back over her entire life, she seemed well-equipped and willing to reduce any man to a shadow of himself. At the same time, Dad had a biting sarcasm that could pierce holes in the most psychologically and emotionally adjusted person. His borderline alcoholism just added to the unhealthy environment in our home.

Not only was my home dysfunctional, but my family was not particularly religious. Mom was a devout Catholic when my parents got married, and a few years into their marriage, Dad surprised her by becoming Catholic. He found reasons (fabricated or otherwise) to leave the house and attend RCIA classes. We did say grace before meals, and I remember reciting the classic children's prayer "Now I Lay Me Down to Sleep" every evening in our living room.

Undoubtedly, the main religious figure in my family was my uncle, a Redemptorist priest. Though he was sent to Thailand immediately after his ordination, he tried to make annual trips to the United States to see us and many of his friends and benefactors. Many of our Christmases were filled with gifts thanks to his generosity. He would regularly record messages to us (sometimes over a period of days or weeks, depending on his schedule) on cassette tapes, and we would listen to them around the dinner table. By means of my uncle's visits and his letters and tapes, I managed to have a closer connection to our Catholic Faith than I might have had otherwise. I especially appreciated my uncle's love, generosity, and spiritual example following my parents' divorce.

We children and our mom got on with life without our dad. He was absolutely faithful to his alimony and child support payments. For that, we all owe him a huge debt of gratitude. My mom still had to work multiple jobs at times just to earn the rest of the money we needed to have some semblance of a decent life.

Shortly after the divorce, both of my parents remarried. Our first stepdad died of lung cancer within a few years. Mom married again, but that relationship didn't last for very long, either. Dad got remarried to a woman whose two kids had been taken away and raised in a state-run facility because she had been deemed unfit to care for them. She was sweet enough but had her share of psychological and emotional issues.

The few times we made arrangements to visit Dad, I could see that he was a defeated man, beaten down by the failures of his life. Even though he lived within a mile of a Catholic parish, he stopped going to Mass altogether. I know in my heart that he never stopped believing in the truth of the Faith. I think he became so consumed by shame that his perceived unworthiness caused him to stay away from the sacraments.

Having always been a diligent worker, Dad entered a living hell when he finally had to retire. He was home every day and, as far as I know, didn't leave his apartment, except perhaps for some grocery shopping or beer runs. He would sit in his apartment and drink while his wife yelled at him, getting on his nerves and sometimes even throwing cans of food at him. It is truly hard to believe how he could have led such a life. Somehow, he managed to find a way to make it from one day to the next.

In early 1996, I received word that Dad was in the hospital with congestive heart failure, the result of decades spent smoking and drinking. Thankfully, I was able to take several days off work to make the trip back to Seattle to see him — truthfully, to say goodbye to him. Since I really didn't know Dad, I had many questions: What was I supposed to say? Should I hug him? Should I tell him I love him? Should I say I've been searching for him all my life? Should I tell him what a mess he and Mom made of our family and our lives?

All of us children felt profound discomfort as we struggled to process the impending death of this man, who was largely a stranger to us, and tried to bring some closure to our fractured family. We decided on a strategy to give each of us a little time alone with him: Two of us would walk in and chat for a few minutes. Then, one would make up a reason to leave the room. We did this until we'd all had the opportunity to find something meaningful to say.

Amazingly, while I was in Seattle, Dad's health improved, and he was discharged from the hospital. I returned to my job, unsure whether I would soon be boarding another plane for the Pacific Northwest. Sure enough, it wasn't long before I got another call, this time one indicating that his death was indeed imminent.

This time, there were no words exchanged: Dad was unconscious and barely holding on. Divine Providence allowed all five of us children and Mom to be present as death approached. After all of the heartaches and sadness we had experienced—the broken marriages, the dysfunction at home, the struggles to make sense of life—here we were, surrounding Dad's deathbed as if we had been one big happy family all along. Again, only God could write such a script.

As I watched, the man who helped to create me and bring me into the world took his last breath. I didn't know how to feel. More than anything, I was numb. I had witnessed death before, but Dad's death was different. I seem to remember looking at his corpse and thinking, "Huh. Some man just died." I did cry for about thirty seconds, but that was all the sorrow I had. It's true that we were all together one last time, but the decades of disconnection and estrangement remained.

And yet there is hope in my story: before his death, Dad received the last rites, and he took his last breath while holding a rosary. With such gentleness, our Heavenly Father had welcomed my dad back into His good graces at the very hour of his death.

"Are you kidding me?" I thought. "God, are you serious? How can you be so tender with us when we make such messes of our lives?"

I'd love to be able to say that I helped prepare Dad's path back to God through my fervent daily prayers. Oh, I did pray for him—many, many times. But I didn't think about the state of his soul every day. Because I really never knew Dad, I didn't have any strong emotional attachment to him that might have led me to offer numerous Masses, Rosaries, and Chaplets of Divine Mercy for his well-being and salvation. Yet I felt so very blessed that at the moment Dad needed God more than ever, He saw fit to keep him in the palm of His hand.

The beauty of this story is that while I never really knew Dad, if I persevere to the end, he and I will have all of eternity to spend together—far longer than we had on earth. Sometimes we are deprived of important relationships on this side of Heaven. It can be so easy to believe that there is no hope for our fallen-away loved ones, but there is *always* hope. Our loving and merciful God longs for our loved ones to die in a state of grace. If God brought our family back together at Dad's bedside, how can I ever doubt that He desires to have us all together around His throne, worshipping Him until the end of time? Jesus, may it be so!

More Things Are Wrought through Prayer ...

By Margaret E. von Bingen

∞

My mother would often say in her southern drawl, which she kept even after seventy years of living in the north, "More things are wrought through prayer than this world knows!" She was a prayer warrior with the perseverance of St. Monica. When Mom prayed, God listened! Like the Good Shepherd, if one of her lambs strayed from the Catholic Faith, she would leave the ninety-nine (well, the nine, in our case) to bring back the lost one. Most likely, she'd have the hook of her crook around his neck, instead of carrying him on her shoulders (she was barely five feet tall), but she wouldn't rest until he was safely back in the fold.

William Augustine Prodigalson Jr. was the long-awaited baby boy after several girls. My father's pride and joy, he was the golden child who could do no wrong. At least, not in Dad's eyes. His sisters knew better!

Gus was smart, athletic, outgoing, and popular with the girls. He attended twelve years of Catholic school, served as an altar boy, and even considered the priesthood. An overachiever (it runs in the family), he headed off to an out-of-state university after high school with a full scholarship to study pre-med. I missed him, and I remember trying to stay awake late into the night, eager for him to arrive from his hitchhiking journey home. (Back then, hitchhiking wasn't as dangerous and was a common way for college students to travel.) He joined a fraternity, and I suspect that is where his curiosity about pornography commenced. Recently, I heard that the university he attended was considered a haven of pornography during the era when the industry and culture gained mainstream acceptance.

Gus married a nice Christian girl, a music major, who became a Catholic to marry him but never did understand why, as she put it, "Catholics don't like to sing!" They had a son, William Augustine Prodigalson III. The stress of medical school and residency can be hard on any marriage, but when Gus went outside the marriage for comfort, he and his wife ended up getting divorced. It sent shock waves through the family. Prodigalsons just didn't divorce! Although Mom was more vocal about her disapproval, I think it was Dad, a faithful man of integrity, who was heartbroken the most. The pedestal Dad had Gus on was beginning to totter.

It wasn't long before Gus announced his upcoming "marriage" to his mistress. My parents, wiser than I, didn't attend the wedding. They understood it wouldn't be a valid marriage, since Gus hadn't sought an annulment from the Church regarding his first marriage. Mom prayed.

Regretfully, with a misguided sense of loyalty to my brother, I attended the wedding with my sister. I referred to Gus in my journal as "my brother … a stranger." I didn't know who he was anymore. He assured me that if this marriage didn't work, it would be their own fault, because they could "communicate." As if lack of communication with his first wife had been the problem, and his infidelity and pornography use were irrelevant to the demise of their marriage! Denial is a powerful weapon the Evil One uses to deceive us, and it was alive and well in our family.

There's an old saying that "if they'll do it with you, they'll do it to you." Just as Gus's wife left her husband to be with Gus when he was still married, he left her for someone else. Sadly, they had two children in grade school when their relationship fell apart.

Gus's "wife" had shared with me that in the beginning, she was open to watching porn with him, but as his interest progressed, she became repulsed by it. She even said that Gus acted as if he were high at times after viewing porn. She didn't suspect any drug use, and viewing porn does release chemicals in the brain, such as dopamine, that have addictive effects similar to those of drugs. That may explain why he appeared high. Apparently, by this time, Gus's interest in pornography had become a full-blown addiction. Although my parents were unaware of Gus's involvement with pornography, the pedestal Dad had Gus on was cracking now that he had abandoned yet another family.

At this time, Gus's latest mistress, a stripper named Scarlet, had moved in with him. My heart went out to her when I met her. To me, Scarlet was like a little girl starving for love who had allowed her body to be surgically transformed into an object of use for men. She assured me that she was committed to "taking care of him" so well that "he wouldn't ever leave" her. I found it sad that Scarlet felt she needed to earn his love and didn't see her inherent dignity as a child of God. Dad's pedestal came crashing down when he learned how far Gus had strayed this time.

Even when the situation seemed hopeless, Mom never gave up hope or stopped praying. She told me that she had heard that a bishop told St. Monica to "talk less to your son about God and more to God about your son!" Mom was convinced that God would answer her prayers and bring Gus back to the Catholic Faith. Although he lived out of state and was a busy, successful surgeon, I think Gus was too ashamed by this time to come home, and so he rarely visited. Call it the inspiration of the Holy Spirit or just a crazy idea of mine: I decided to go visit him. I had a plan!

I had obtained a large print of the Divine Mercy image from some sisters of St. Faustina's order in Poland, whom I had met when they were visiting the United States. When I framed the image, I slipped a blessed Green Scapular between the print and the back of the frame. The Green Scapular is a sacramental approved by Pope Pius IX in 1870. It does not need to be worn by the person for whom the graces of conversion are desired, only to be in his presence. There is a prayer — "Immaculate Heart of Mary, pray for us, now and at the hour of our death" — that is to be said daily either by the person seeking the graces or by another on his behalf.

When I visited Gus and Scarlet, I gave them the Divine Mercy picture. Gus received it politely, but Scarlet really seemed drawn to it and hung it up in a prominent place in the house while I was there. Mom was the only one I had told about what I had done, and we faithfully prayed the Green Scapular prayer daily for Scarlet and Gus.

About a year or so later, I heard that Scarlet had left Gus. Once again, "if they'll do it with you, they'll do it to you." This time, he was on the receiving end, and he was not doing well. In the depths of despair, he hit rock bottom. He called me out of the blue and asked me if I had gone to Medjugorje. He had come across and then read a book on Medjugorje I had given him at least ten years earlier. I told him I had been to Medjugorje and that Mom and I were planning to go to Ireland soon. I knew the spiritual director of an Irish visionary there. I asked Gus if he would like to go with us. Perhaps it was curiosity, or maybe the grace of the Holy Spirit, but after coming up with a variety of excuses he reluctantly accepted my invitation. He told me later that a family member had told him Mom and I were going to Ireland, and he had asked, "Why would they want to do that?"

I think the trip to Ireland was transformative for him. We visited many churches and attended a Mass celebrated by the spiritual director I knew. That Mass was especially moving, as the celebrant experienced some spiritual gifts during the Consecration. I will always treasure that time spent with my mom and brother. After we returned, while visiting my parents in Florida, we were telling the Irish pastor of my parents' parish about our trip. Gus tilted his head and glanced at me as he said in an accusatory tone, "She took me there to convert me." I thought I was busted. I was nervously waiting for what he would say next, when he broke into a smile and said, "It worked!"

On a visit to Gus's home, after he returned to his Catholic Faith and became a daily communicant, I was looking through his now-unlocked collection of VHS tapes. One video was labeled "Mother Angelica Live," but I could see something partially erased underneath the title. Looking closer, I realized it was the title of a porn video. Gus admitted that he had taped EWTN programs over all of his porn flicks! The prodigal son had come home!

I have to admit that the biblical story of the prodigal son usually left me feeling sympathetic toward the faithful older son. Having always been very committed to my Catholic Faith, I could identify more closely with him than with the younger son. However, I truly rejoiced when my brother returned to the Faith, and I gained a new perspective after sharing part of his journey home. I realized that although forgiven through the mercy of God, he will still live the rest of his life with the effects of his sinful choices, especially those that affected his children so deeply. I decided to keep my cross: it fits me, and his would be much too heavy for me to bear!

Pornography is ubiquitous today, especially in the digital world. Many claim watching porn is a personal, private choice that doesn't affect others. I believe that as a result of porn addictions, there are thousands of children growing up without their fathers in their homes who would strongly disagree with that claim. Pornography destroys marriages, families, and ultimately the addicted person. There is always hope, through the mercy of Jesus Christ, as evidenced by my brother's journey. If you or someone you love struggles with pornography, there are faith-based resources listed at the end of this story that may be helpful.

What do I hope you take away from this story? Firstly, never give up hope! With God, all things are possible! Fast and pray. Persevere as my mom and St. Monica did and remember to "talk less to your loved one about God and more to God about your loved one." While your loved one may not be open to what you have to say, God is always open to hearing your concerns, and He can respond far more powerfully than we can.

Secondly, never underestimate the effects of the seeds you plant, even if they seem dormant for years. The book on Medjugorje collected dust on Gus's bookshelf for over a decade! Yet it was there when he was finally ready to receive the hope it contained. God's timing is perfect.

Finally, we have a powerful Mother in Heaven who is just waiting for us to ask her for help. The Rosary is the most powerful prayer we have, next to the Mass. I know that my mom and I prayed many Rosaries, and I suspect that my dad prayed more than a few in his own quiet way.

And now, to quote Paul Harvey, for "the rest of the story": shortly after my brother returned to the Faith, my sister, who lived in the Bible Belt, announced that she had left the Catholic Church to join a so-called Bible-believing church. My heart broke for Mom, as her happiness at having all of her lambs back in the fold was short-lived. Although she prayed for another twenty years for my sister and watched EWTN's *The Journey Home* religiously, Mom did not live to see her return to the Catholic Faith. But Mom was never at a loss for words, so I'm sure God is getting an earful in Heaven about my sister (think of the judge and the persistent widow in Luke 18:1–8). I trust that all things are possible with God!

Resources for battling pornography

- **CovenantEyes.com**: Accountability software.
- **AriseForHim.com**: Monica Breaux, Ph.D., offers programs for men addicted to pornography: Wholly Men, for adults, and Wholly Teens, for teenagers. Wholly Women is for female partners of men with porn addictions. Dr. Breaux also offers tools for prevention and for priests to use in Confession.
- **MattFradd.com**: Matt Fradd, a best-selling Catholic author and the host of the *Pints with Aquinas* podcast, offers STRIVE, an anonymous twenty-one-day detox program for those who struggle with porn addiction.

This Is for You

By Mary Walton

∞

This is not the story of a prodigal son, but of a prodigal daughter. It does not have a happy ending. I'm still traveling on this heartbreaking, pain-filled journey. In hopes of reaching someone on a similar path, I'd like to share how my family's journey began and where we are today.

My husband and I raised our daughter Lucy and her brother in a loving Catholic home. Don't get me wrong, we weren't perfect, but we were good parents. We took our kids to Mass every week and prayed before every meal. As a stay-at-home mom, I drove the kids to and from school and extracurricular activities every day, praying and singing with them in the car. I helped my kids with homework and volunteered regularly at their schools. I read to them at night and prayed with them before bed. Their dad was right there with me, being available for them and giving them time, attention, and spiritual guidance. And they had two loving grandmothers to dote on them.

This all sounds cozy and wonderful, doesn't it? You'd expect everything to turn out okay. But it didn't.

Lucy was always a curious, skeptical, strong-willed child: if we told her that the sky was blue, she would counter that it was green. She could never take our word for anything, and we had to be firm to keep her in check. One memorable incident occurred when Lucy was helping me bake (she was about nine years old at the time).

"The cinnamon smells so good," she said. "I want to taste it!"

"It'll taste good once we've finished baking," I said, "but it'll taste awful if you eat it raw."

Of course, Lucy had to try it. When my back was turned, she put an entire tablespoon of cinnamon in her mouth, only to end up choking and trying to spit it out.

It was like that with her every step of the way. She rebelled and fought with us over nearly everything. She was a great student, but often socially awkward and always drawn to the bizarre and troubled kids in school. We'd caution her about getting involved with kids who were known to be trouble, but she couldn't seem to help herself. We kept her busy with extracurricular activities, but never busy enough. Unfortunately, we couldn't fill up her schedule with youth group or other parish activities. You see, we live in a rural area where there are few Catholics. Our parish is tiny. On top of that, let's just say the diocese usually didn't send us the best priests. We've had tyrants and liberals who made even me want to walk out of Mass. You can imagine what their lackluster witness did to the faith of my children.

When Lucy was about fifteen, she started going out with a Protestant boy. Foolishly, I didn't think too much about their relationship. In fact, I was glad she'd found a Christian boyfriend: at least Jesus could be in the picture. Looking back now, I realize how naïve I was. Back in the day, when I was growing up, all my friends and family were Catholic; I didn't really know anyone who was Protestant. The nuns at my school talked little about the long-standing divide between the Catholic Church and the Protestant denominations. So when Lucy met this boy,

I was unprepared for the challenge he and his church could pose to her faith. I was especially unprepared for her to meet Protestants who had once been Catholic. Thinking about it now, I foolishly believed that my children would never leave the Faith, since I'd never so much as thought about questioning the Church. My Faith had always been a part of who I was. That's why I didn't notice that by the time Lucy met this boy, she had already stopped believing in the Catholic Faith. When we went to Mass together, when we prayed as a family, she was just playing along. And it was about to get worse: Lucy had just been accepted to college.

Ah, college. The years I now refer to as the "indoctrination years." How unprepared my husband and I were for the evil that now stalks our college campuses. Most parents are blind to what has become, for me, a familiar scene: these "wonderful professors" serving our young, impressionable children a golden chalice filled with atheist, liberal Kool-Aid. When our kids are urged to "drink up," they do, and then there is no turning back.

I still remember the dread I felt when Lucy came dancing into our bedroom to show us her acceptance letter. I just had a terrible feeling in my heart. I knew something bad was coming.

"I just don't think Lucy should go to this school," I told my husband that night. "I don't think it will be good for her."

"I know how you feel," he said. "Maybe it'll be good for her after all. It's a famous school, so she'll have a shot at getting a good job once she graduates."

As it turns out, we were both correct. Lucy did find a good job in Washington, DC. But she completely turned her back on the Faith.

During her junior year, Lucy lived in a sorority house. She had a Jewish roommate named Sarah. Often, the two of them went to parties at the Jewish fraternity house next door, where Lucy made lots of male friends. We encouraged her to befriend some kids from the college's Catholic campus ministry, but she had plenty of excuses.

"They're boring," she'd tell us. "They seem snobbish to me."

Long story short, she soon started dating a Jewish boy. Truthfully, he was a good guy. His mom was Jewish, and his dad had been raised Christian. Even though his family didn't practice much of anything anymore, this boy had at least been exposed to Christianity, and he respected the Christian Faith.

When we visited Lucy for her college's family weekend, we took her and her boyfriend out to dinner. While we were eating, I overheard them practicing some Hebrew words together, and I became suspicious. After we dropped her boyfriend off at his fraternity house, we sat Lucy down in her room.

"What's going on?" I asked.

That's when we found out Lucy had swapped Sunday Mass for weekly worship at the local synagogue. Our daughter now considered herself Jewish and had abandoned her Catholic Faith.

Thus began the hellish journey we are now on. I can't describe to you the shock, despair, and sense of betrayal I felt. It was hard not to blame myself, especially when I met Sarah's mom, Judith, who had also come to visit for the weekend. Judith admired Lucy's determination to choose her own religion and forge her own path. In turn, Lucy looked up to Judith, who was an accomplished businesswoman, while I was just a "boring" stay-at-home mom.

"Who does this?" I kept asking. "What happened? Did we do something wrong?"

It didn't matter. Our daughter was Jewish, and that was that. She told us she'd never go to a Catholic church again. She was happy going to services at the Reconstructionist temple, where she could believe what she wanted to believe and pray however she wanted to pray.

"We can even do yoga there if we want!" she once told us gleefully.

But Lucy's open-mindedness only went so far. She had sure closed her mind to Catholicism. Once, her dad tried to have a patient, sincere conversation with her about the Faith. She just went off the deep end and screamed at him, "You can die and I'll still never be a Catholic ever again!"

Of course, this whole thing had now taken over my mind and my life. I was consumed with anger, and I couldn't focus on anything else. Then, one day, I saw on our kitchen counter a pamphlet entitled *How to Pray the Rosary*. Every time I walked by, I seemed to feel Mary's presence. I prayed every day, but I'd gotten out of the habit of saying the Rosary. With Mary's gentle encouragement, I decided to dedicate myself to the Rosary again. Today, I pray it every day for Lucy, that she find her way home to the Church.

Once I began praying the Rosary, Mary showed me other ways of practicing the Faith. My husband, who is on the road frequently, had started listening to EWTN in the car. He suggested I tune in as well.

"I don't know," I said. "It sounds like it'll just be a lot of organ music and sermons."

"It's not," he said. "It's fascinating. You'd enjoy it."

Reluctantly, I decided to give EWTN a try. Once I overcame my resistance, I was hooked. I started listening to *The Doctor Is In* with Dr. Ray Guarendi; then, I became obsessed with *The Journey Home* with Marcus Grodi. I felt so drawn to EWTN: every program was about real people like me with real problems like mine. I took comfort in their stories. So many of the women featured on EWTN reminded me of Lucy. Like her, they were educated and used to think of themselves as too smart for religion.

"If these women could come back to the Faith," I thought, "maybe Lucy could, too."

My husband and I started listening to *Take 2 with Jerry and Debbie*. Before long, I was pouring out my heart to Debbie in an email. I called in to the show to talk about how parents can keep their kids from leaving the Faith in college. During that phone call, I heard about a book by Roy Schoeman called *Salvation Is from the Jews*. Schoeman's book, especially its stories of Jews who became Catholic, gave me hope.

Around this time, things went from bad to worse with Lucy. She decided to take a job with the military. When she first told us, I supported her decision, until she casually mentioned a crucial detail: she'd be working overseas in an unsafe country. I came completely unglued, but I couldn't change her mind. That's just how she is. While I worried about her safety, she moved to an unfriendly country; while I prayed for her soul, she made glib comments, such as, "Maybe I'll wind up dying and find that I was wrong about everything all along."

I decided to slip a copy of Roy Schoeman's book into Lucy's suitcase, along with a loving letter explaining how much I'd enjoyed the book and asking her to consider reading it. Sadly, when she found the book and read my letter, Lucy exploded. She sent me a hateful text message threatening to cut me out of her life if I ever did anything like this again.

I felt like I'd been stabbed in the heart. I wept bitterly. But after I pulled myself together, I knew I couldn't handle things anymore. I'd have to turn my problems over to God—completely.

I told Him that I could no longer handle the exhaustion and heartbreak my daughter had caused me. When I made up my mind and heart to give my suffering to God, I felt a sense of peace come over me. That peace has remained with me for years now.

I don't mean to say that my life got better all at once. I still have bad days; I still experience moments of grief, but little by little, God has given me strength. He has a way of giving you what He thinks you need. Sometimes, I seem to hear Him whispering, "This is for you."

I realize now that God has called me to spiritual boot camp! All my life, I was Catholic, and yes, I practiced my Faith. But I've learned it's not enough. We need to be strengthened and forged by fire. As much as we'd like to avoid trials, they strengthen us.

Fortunately, we don't have to struggle all alone. I know I can't thank my husband enough for being a pillar of strength during this trial. He's always there for me and never loses his faith in God. I'm eternally grateful, too, for Mother Angelica and everyone at EWTN, especially Debbie. These wonderful people keep the Faith going, despite the trials they have all had to overcome.

I advise the many Catholic parents who have prodigal children to pray. Pray the Rosary and devote yourself to Mary. Talk to God constantly. Ask for the intercession of the angels and saints (especially St. Monica, St. Augustine, and St. Padre Pio). These practices have helped me immensely.

Remember, too, that you probably can't change your child's mind. Try not to get into dead-end arguments or go off the deep end. Of course, each child is different. Not everyone has a wildcat like Lucy.

My daughter remains as rebellious and defiant as ever. I've often told God, "Dear Lord, if you can nudge her along, show her the way, and get her back on the path to you, you will have a strong warrior to defend you and the Faith. She's a force to be reckoned with and doesn't buckle easily. She'd pass your boot camp with flying colors!"

What a story it will be when my prodigal daughter comes home.

1 Corinthians 8:13

By Al Joseph

∞

Imagine you've been invited to an event at your parish. Maybe it's an annual dinner, an ice cream social, or a mission—you get the idea. You're looking forward to spending some time with your fellow parishioners, people who share your beliefs and your values.

When you pull into the parking lot and join the crowd, you see everyone laughing and having a good time. You notice that almost everyone is wearing the same T-shirt. "That's kind of neat," you think. "Maybe I can get one."

But then, someone turns around to say hello, and you see the words "I Love Planned Parenthood" on the front of the shirt.

You hurry to ask your pastor what's going on. When you find him, you're shocked to see that not only is he wearing one of the T-shirts, but he's helping distribute them.

You and your pastor have the following exchange:

You: Hey, Father. The Church says abortion is wrong. Doesn't that mean we're against abortion?

Your pastor: Well, of course we're against it.

You: So what's up with the shirts?

Your pastor: Oh, just because the Church says abortion is wrong doesn't mean we can't wear T-shirts in support of Planned Parenthood. They're very comfy. You're a large, right?

Imagine how you'd feel. Now keep that feeling in mind. We'll come back to this shocking, confusing scene, but first, let me tell you my story.

My life has been shaped by two constants: my Catholic Faith and my love for animals. I grew up a practicing Catholic. My parents instilled in me a deep love for God and the Church. My whole family, including my Protestant mom, went to Mass every Sunday and holy day. My dad, a cradle Catholic, would often read stories from a children's Bible to my sister and me. We said prayers every night and attended Sunday school after Mass. My sister and I attended Catholic high schools. As a teenager, I even considered becoming a priest, though I eventually saw that God had other plans for my life.

Just as I have always loved God (well, almost always), I have always cared for animals. In my baby book, my mom wrote that I "liked any story pertaining to animals, especially dogs." Growing up, I loved to watch any show with animals, especially *Lassie*. I also liked Tarzan. Not only did he have a special bond with animals, but he protected them. I kept turtles, fish, and other small animals as pets, but I was closest to our dog, who filled my life with joy. Every summer, I visited my grandparents' farm, where I spent many happy hours with the cows and dogs and chickens and pigs.

That was my life, until I graduated from high school and left for college. Away from home for the first time, I began to question myself. What did I mean when I said I loved animals, and who was this God I'd been praying to all this time?

As I asked these questions, I began exploring different ways of thinking and living. I took philosophy classes, where we were told to leave God outside the classroom. I started looking into Hinduism and Buddhism and New Age spirituality. But the biggest influence on me at that time was Albert Schweitzer and his "Reverence for Life" philosophy. Essentially, Schweitzer believed that all living things want to live, and so we must not kill unnecessarily.

In Schweitzer's philosophy and in the other faiths I studied, I found a deep concern for animals that was missing from Catholicism. I began to doubt my childhood Faith. The Church was wrong about animals and animal rights; what else was She wrong about?

Before long, I stopped attending Mass, except when I went home during school breaks. I ignored God, unless I had an emergency. I figured He would bail me out if I needed Him, but I didn't realize He was always there, looking out for me every day of my life.

After college, I met a woman. We started living together, and soon, we were talking about marriage.

"We have to get married in a Catholic church," I said. "I don't want to upset my dad."

We had to shop around for a priest—not only were we living together, but my fiancée and I had no plans of having children—but eventually, we got married in the Church. After nine years, my wife's biological clock started ticking. Still, I refused to have a child.

"Our dogs and cats are our kids," I said.

Then, something changed. I felt something old and familiar stirring inside me. I know now that it was the Holy Spirit, calling me to abandon my selfishness. Finally, I gave in, and my wife and I had a daughter.

Everything changed when Clare was born. Not right away, and not without starts and stops, but I started thinking about God more. I began praying (even when there wasn't an emergency). Soon, I was attending Mass again.

All of this was hard on my wife. Not only did she have a new kid, with all the joys and pressures that brings, but I was becoming a stranger to her. My wife had been raised Catholic, but we'd both stopped practicing the Faith long before we met. You can imagine how her world seemed askew. But God was working in her too: she agreed to raise Clare in the Faith.

Clare attended Catholic school from kindergarten through high school. We prayed together and never missed Mass. We talked about how much God loves us. We talked about apologetics, ethics, and Catholic social teaching. We also talked about animals: how much God loves them, what the Bible and the *Catechism* say about them, and why we call them our brothers and sisters (as St. Francis taught).

For a long time, Clare shared my love for God and animals. She was raised a vegetarian and later chose to be vegan. Ever the activist, she tried to educate her friends and classmates when they questioned her, and she would never back down from her beliefs, even when other kids made fun of her.

Unfortunately, things fell apart. When Clare was twelve, my wife and I divorced. We've been anywhere from civil to friendly with each other, which has made our separation easier, but I know it was still hard on Clare.

Then, in her junior year of high school, Clare slowly stopped caring about her Faith. She paid little attention during Mass. When we shared with each other one thing we heard God saying to us during the readings — a longstanding practice of ours — Clare would say, "We should love God," over and over, like a broken record.

Then, one day, Clare told me she would no longer go to Mass.

My heart just broke. I felt as if my daughter had rejected me and severed our relationship. I prayed through tears of fear and worry.

For a while, I went through the grieving process, battling denial and anger. I turned to St. Monica for help. Slowly, God gave me hope. He showed me that He loves Clare more than I ever could. He would take care of her and guide her.

Eventually, Clare and I were able to talk about why she left the Church. Surprise, surprise: like me, she left over the animal issue. Clare believes it is wrong to kill or harm animals needlessly, yet she sees priests doing so all the time.

"Priests are our moral guides," she told me. "If they can be so wrong about animals, how can I trust them on anything else?"

Sound familiar?

I tried everything to help Clare rethink her decision to leave the Church. Once, I invited her to attend a talk at our parish with me. The talk would be about something she enjoyed, and I thought the speaker might be able to open a door back to the Faith for Clare. Wanting to make me happy, she agreed to attend.

When we arrived, everyone was laughing and having a good time. I saw lots of people around Clare's age, which made me hopeful—maybe she'd find some good Catholic friends. I couldn't help but smile. Things might be okay after all.

Then, we noticed that almost everyone was eating hamburgers and hot dogs. The last three popes have said that factory farming is cruel and evil, but here we were, watching parishioners and priests enjoy the product of that cruelty, as if to say, "Oh, just because the Church says animal cruelty is wrong doesn't mean we can't enjoy meat. Here, have a hamburger!"

I know you might not understand Clare's feelings, but I'd like you to try. Remember how you felt when I asked you to imagine your pastor wearing a Planned Parenthood T-shirt? Remember the pain, the outrage, the shock? Wouldn't you feel betrayed? That's just what Clare and I felt. The door I wanted to open for her slammed shut in her face. My fine plan came to a screeching halt.

More often than not, this is what happens when our loved ones leave the Church. They perceive something that scandalizes them. For Clare, it was the blind eye Catholics turned to animal cruelty. For your loved one, it may be discrimination, abuse, or some other injustice. It is so hard to get our loved ones to believe in Jesus, whom they can't see, when they can see so many problems, real or imagined, in the Church.

Maybe our loved ones don't have understandable reasons for leaving. Maybe they do. Either way, if we want any chance of bringing them back to the Faith, we need to work hard to understand their thoughts and feelings. We also need to be careful to set a good example so that we do not push our loved ones even further from the Church. St. Paul put it this way: "If food causes my brother to sin, I will never eat meat again, so that I may not cause my brother to sin" (1 Cor. 8:13).

Now, I am not quoting this to say you should never eat meat again (that's an argument for another time). Instead, I want you to ask yourself, "What 'meat' do I enjoy that might be keeping someone from returning to the Church?" I do not at all mean to say we should water down or change the Church's teachings. But maybe you love winning arguments and rubbing your victories in people's faces. Maybe you struggle with pride and anger. We all have bad habits that just aren't worth losing souls over. Can you give that up? Can you keep the door open, instead of slamming it? I urge you to consider this.

Now, let me share some things I wish I would have done to help Clare stay in the Church.

First, I would have worked harder at being a selfless husband and father. My divorce is a huge burden for Clare, one she wouldn't have to carry had I done more to save my marriage.

Second, I would have spent more time with our parish priests, so Clare would have known them as friends and would have felt comfortable talking with them about her concerns. It's also important for us all to remember that our leaders are human and imperfect. When scandals come to light, as they will, we won't be caught quite so off guard.

In the same vein, I would have talked more about God's mercy. Catholic or not, we all make mistakes, but in the Church, we can experience God's forgiveness and compassion. Though the world can be cruel, we can find healing in the sacraments.

Finally, I would have paid more attention to what my daughter was learning (or not learning) in school. Catholic education is fantastic, but individual teachers can give kids the wrong ideas. Just as importantly, kids sometimes think they know everything about the Faith just because they've taken a few religion classes.

To illustrate this point, let me return to my own conversion story. When I left the Faith, I was convinced that the Church didn't care about animals. I came to that conclusion after studying non-Catholic traditions. Since I thought I already knew everything there was to know about Catholicism, I didn't see the point of studying the *Catechism* or the Bible to see what the Church actually taught about reverence for life. Then, when Clare was born and I felt my conscience nagging me, I realized what an oversight I'd made. I needed to know what the Church taught if I wanted to raise my daughter as a Catholic. I picked up the *Catechism*, and there it was, staring me in the face: "It is contrary to human dignity to cause animals to suffer or die needlessly" (CCC 2418).

In the words of the great Homer Simpson: "D'oh!"

I thought I knew everything about the Faith. How could I have missed such a crucial piece of information? When I read the Bible, the lives of the saints, and Church documents, I found the same message of respect for animals. And the more I read, the more I wanted to know God and be close to Him. In His mysterious way, God used the very reason I had left the Faith to bring me back home. In fact, if I hadn't left the Church, I might never have come to love and know God as much as I do now.

So take heart. God can redeem any situation, no matter how hopeless it may seem. Never forget how much God loves your loved ones. He will work tirelessly to bring them home.

It has been a few years since Clare left the Church. We're blessed to have a close relationship. Both of us work for an organization that protects animals. We can talk about God and the Church.

I pray for my daughter every day. I rely on the Rosary, regular adoration, daily Mass, and the intercessions of St. Monica and St. Francis. Mostly, I just reflect on God's great love for Clare. He's working to bring her home, so that one day, just like her dad, she can look back and say, "D'oh!"

The Search for God

By Isabella de la Cruz

∞

My older brother Vincente is my best friend. He has always been my anchor, and often, he is my voice of reason. We speak nearly every day—over the phone, in person, or via text—and have no problem saying, "I love you."

But after my brother left the Faith to join the Pentecostal church, anger crept into his heart like a dark fog. For years, we clashed over his rejection of the Catholic Church. To me, rejecting the Faith meant rejecting the very Catholic family in which Vincente, our younger brother Antonio, and I grew up. We had a huge Bible in the center of our living room, and on the wall was a crucifix four feet tall. My mother carried it with her on an airplane from Mexico. Beneath the crucifix was a tall, skinny white table used as an altar.

Family dinners were sacred, ceremonial occasions. As she cooked, my mother would make the Sign of the Cross over the food with whatever utensil she had in hand. We blessed our food as a family before we ate. Afterward, we knelt down and prayed the Rosary together.

Every morning, my mother would bless us before we left for school. She would make the Sign of the Cross on each of our foreheads with her thumb, place her hands on our heads, and then bow her head toward ours and pray for our protection. She would finish the blessing by making the Sign of the Cross once again over our foreheads, then our lips, and then our hearts. While doing this, she would recite the following prayer in Spanish: "By the Sign of the Holy Cross, from our enemies protect us, Lord our God. Amen."

We also went to Mass every Sunday, and during the week, my mother would sometimes take us to local charismatic prayer sessions. Occasionally, she also took us to healing Masses. At one of these Masses, someone in the crowd, possessed by demons, fell to the ground. My mother covered my eyes and ears with her hands.

Vincente, however, witnessed the entire ordeal. He described to me the different voices and sounds coming from the possessed person, whose body kept twisting and contorting. He was fascinated by the heroic, fearless priest who expelled all the demons. That didn't surprise me: Vincente deeply admired priests and always talked about becoming one someday.

My older brother was certainly the saintliest of us all. His many beautiful drawings and paintings of Mary and the saints made his love for the Faith evident. Vincente was a perceptive artist. My mother realized his gift when, as a toddler, he picked up a pencil, found a blank page in our family Bible, and drew a profile of a face that took up the entire page. There were two dynamic aspects of the finished drawing. First, he had formed a perfect profile out of a conglomerate of squiggly lines, and second, the squiggly lines never disconnected. One continuous line formed the perfect profile. Again, he was a toddler when he did this!

Vincente taught me that artists are always searching for something that reveals the deep essence of life, love, and faith. He seemed to have an unusually rich awareness of God's love and presence, and he was always longing for a deeper relationship with God.

Unfortunately, for reasons I don't fully understand, Vincente began to believe he had to look for God outside the Catholic Faith. In his early twenties, Vincente was introduced to Buddhism, which was touted as a spiritual practice that could be incorporated into any religion. Soon, Vincente perceived that Buddhism was incompatible with Christianity. He immediately stopped practicing Buddhism and resolved never to explore non-Christian religions or philosophies. But still he searched. He tried out different Christian denominations, but none moved him, until one day, he walked into a Pentecostal church. He declared that he had found the true church at last. Soon, his pastor noticed his devotion and invited him to preach at services. A magnificent storyteller, Vincente convinced many people to deepen their faith and follow God.

Before long, Vincente had begun to try to win our family over to Pentecostalism. Armed with the typical Protestant arguments against the Catholic Church, he would kindly tell me that I belonged to the wrong faith. He said that having statues of saints was idolatry, or that Catholics didn't know enough about the Bible, or that the only "Holy Father" we needed was God, not a wicked pope.

Our family mourned the loss of our saintly future priest to Protestantism. He could have become a staunch defender of the Faith; instead, he was using his intellect and years of biblical studies to tear the Church down. It was especially difficult to hear Vincente criticize our devotion to Mary. He had once loved her so much, and now he couldn't have a conversation without criticizing her. One day, Vincente became so heated and so insistent that my father warned him never to call again unless he could stop demeaning Our Lady. Vincente eased up after that, but he kept inviting us to attend his church with him.

Finally, I decided to go to a service with Vincente, partly to make him happy, but mostly because I wanted a chance to hold his little girl, my niece. All during the service, people chanted, stomped, cried, and danced. The chaos made me uncomfortable.

Once it was over, the congregation met in the church dining hall. A man holding a Bible came up to me and started haranguing me for my Catholic Faith. He pointed out verses that disproved Mary's perpetual virginity, and then, using biblical numerology, he told me that Satan resided within the Catholic Church.

I never returned to that church. I was hurt, but beneath my anger was a growing awareness that I didn't know my Faith. I didn't know enough about the Bible or about theology to defend the Church to that man.

As I wrestled with this realization, Vincente became angrier not only with my family but with any Catholic he met. Antonio told me that one time, when he was out for a walk with our brother, they saw a statue of Mary in someone's garden. Vincente stormed up to the front door and began berating the woman who answered.

Not long after, my mother showed me a research binder Vincente had left at my parents' house. This binder contained notes, photos, and essays, all directed at proving the evil of Our Lady. Tears in her eyes, my mother took the binder out to the backyard and burned it. At that moment, I knew I couldn't stay silent anymore. Not amidst this spiritual warfare.

I vowed to learn everything I could about my Faith to prepare for the next round of debates with my brother. I didn't want to win the arguments; I wanted to win *him* back.

After some research, I discovered Catholic Answers. I began attending their seminars, reading books, and listening to Catholic radio. I took a course from the Catholic Apologetics Academy, where I learned from Patrick Madrid and his team of apologists. The turning point in my search came when I decided to fast every day during Lent and to pray the Divine Office every three hours. God's love filled my heart, and I was overcome by His presence. I fell deeply in love with my Faith. Now I was ready to face my brother.

The next time I went over to Vincente's house, he challenged my devotion to Mary. Confidently, I pointed out that Mary's role as the Mother of God is foreshadowed throughout the Old Testament, beginning with Genesis.

He cut me off before I could finish my argument and told me to get out. When I refused to leave, Vincente told me I was no longer his sister. He accused me of learning about the Faith just so I could fight with him. I was hurt and sad, but I trusted that our love for each other would ultimately win. Indeed, it didn't take us long to mend things, and since then, he has never challenged me again.

Today, Vincente doesn't go to church at all, but I know he still loves God. My brother remains a prayerful, chaste, and holy man. He is still my best friend, my anchor, and my voice of reason. Whenever I need prayers, he calls on Jesus in the most beautiful way. It brings me to tears. Oh, he would make a great priest. We need him in the Church more than ever now, as wicked priests drive away many of the faithful who, like Vincente, are sincerely searching for God.

As J. R. R. Tolkien famously wrote, "Not all who wander are lost." My brother is not lost. God will bring him home when the time is right. Until then, I will devote myself to prayer and to my love for God and my family. When divisions threaten us, we must love each other all the more. But we must never abandon our Faith. Instead, we must seek to understand it better, so we can be loving witnesses to that truth for which so many people search night and day.

Please pray for my brother. Trust me, you want him on our side.

"What's Love Got to Do with It?"

By Michele Salvatore

∞

My husband, Steve, is the youngest of five children. He was born to an Italian Catholic family in Upstate New York. Unfortunately, his family didn't stay together long: when Steve was in kindergarten, his mother became pregnant with another man's baby. Steve's father was hurt, betrayed, and humiliated, especially when he discovered that the father of the baby was one of his close friends. He decided to divorce his wife and move across the country with Steve and his four siblings.

Steve's father escaped the shame of his wife's infidelity, but, having left his thriving business behind in New York, he had to work multiple jobs to support his children. Because the family moved often, Steve never felt settled or at ease. Like his older siblings, he had to grow up quickly in order to take care of himself.

Shortly after Steve received his First Communion, his family stopped attending Mass. Without any faith to guide him, Steve became restless. He spent years longing for something, though he didn't know what. The one thing that made him feel secure was playing basketball. When his coaches told him he was talented enough to play professionally, Steve dedicated himself fiercely to this goal.

One of Steve's teammates, Don, happened to be a devout Christian. One day, Don invited Steve to attend church with him and his family. Steve admired and trusted Don, and so he agreed. Don introduced Steve to the Scriptures and helped him grow as a Christian and as a young man. Though a baptized Catholic, Steve soon felt at home in this nondenominational community. He was grateful to Don for introducing him to Christianity and for his friendship, which continues to this day.

Unfortunately, Steve never fulfilled his dream of playing professional basketball because the time had come for him to leave home, become an independent man, and earn a living. Encouraged by his father, Steve went into real estate and began a successful career. Eventually, he got married to a woman named Anna.

Steve remained committed to his faith. He took comfort in Scripture and took time every day to thank God for his blessings. But Anna didn't share his commitment, and after thirteen years, their marriage ended in divorce. Steve found himself starting over at forty-two years old, with no marriage, no kids, and no real church to belong to.

Maybe it was Steve's loneliness that led our neighbor Amelia to introduce him to me. She barely knew either of us, and so her suggestion struck me as odd. But I decided to go over to Steve's house, just to say hello. We quickly realized how much we had in common: we were both from the East Coast, we were both Italian, and we were both raised in big Catholic families. From these commonalities, a genuine friendship grew. Before long, my mom had practically adopted Steve into our family!

I can see now that it was the Holy Spirit Who inspired me to share with Steve my love for the Faith. I told him how important the Church was to me, and I asked him if he would join me at Mass. He thought about it for a moment.

"It'd make my dad happy to see me there," Steve said. "He's never said anything, but I think he feels bad about not taking me to church as a kid. I guess I could go."

Everything in Steve's life seemed to come together that Sunday. I can still see the look on his father's face when Steve showed up and sat down beside him. Father and son were bashful but overjoyed as they hugged at the Sign of Peace.

Steve knew God had given him a chance to start over, here, in his true home. He decided to pursue an annulment, which was granted after eighteen months. Around the same time, he told me he wanted to be confirmed. As he went through sacramental preparation, he rediscovered his love for the rich traditions of the Church and Her liturgy.

I was overjoyed when Steve asked me to be his sponsor. When the big day arrived and I stood there before the altar, my hand on Steve's shoulder, I thanked God for bringing him into my life, if only for this moment. I didn't know what the future held for us, but I knew I had done my part to bring the Faith to him, to a man who was once a little boy without a mom or a permanent place to call home. And now here he was, in an unchanging, two-thousand-year-old Church that he knew would never abandon him. He had longed for this his entire life.

God blessed us more than I could have imagined. Not only did He give Steve His Church, but He gave us each other, first as friends, and then as spouses. We've been married for more than ten years now. Oh, and did I mention that Steve is now a fourth-degree Knight of Columbus? How's that for adding a bow and ribbon to the story.

Our journey was so full of moments of grace that I hardly know where to begin. Here are some that stand out to me as I write this.

We truly believe Steve's dad never stopped praying for his children to return to the Faith. He felt responsible for the difficulty and insecurity their family faced, and he hoped his children could find comfort and healing in God, Who had loved them in the face of their suffering. It's so important to recognize that our failings and regrets can never impede the work of God's grace. He will provide, even when we can't, even when we think we may have permanently pushed our loved ones away.

Perhaps the clearest way God provided for Steve was through the people he met. At every moment, Steve was surrounded by people who cared for him and gently led him home. Looking back, we can clearly see how the Holy Spirit handpicked each of these people, putting them in just the right place at the right time. When Steve was a restless, lonely teenager, he met Don, who offered him much-needed comfort and guidance in Scripture and prayer. Amelia introduced Steve and me — two people who should never have met — shortly after his divorce. When Steve saw how much I loved my Faith and how much I wanted him to know God, he was moved to return to the Church. Every priest, deacon, and lay leader Steve encountered during his conversion gave him the exact help he needed to begin his new life in Christ. Even my mom helped Steve learn to love Mary, Our Blessed Mother. Through my mom's care, Steve was able to let Mary heal the wounds of his mom's infidelity. He is now devoted to the Rosary.

Truly, these loving relationships are instrumental to conversion. All too often, people are afraid to share the Faith with each other, but our silence prevents us from leading others to God. We need to be comfortable with discussing what God means to us and inviting others to know Him.

All this is to say: neither doubt the efficacy of your prayers nor ever underestimate the power of your witness. I encourage you to pray that God will introduce the right people to your fallen-away loved ones. We are living proof that He will answer your prayers. Love will bring the lost home.

Lessons Learned on the
St. Joseph Parkway

By Mary Loretta Johnson

∞

With the help of the Holy Spirit and a glass of wine, I hope to tell you the story of my heartache and how it has brought me closer to Jesus.

I have always been in love with my Catholic Faith. As a little girl, I was captivated by the beauty of the liturgy: the flickering candles, the glorious hymns, the melodious bells, the curling smoke rising from the incense. Along with loving the rituals of the Mass, I loved the Bible and stories of the saints. One of my earliest memories is riding in the backseat of my grandpa's car next to an elderly Franciscan priest named Fr. Clem. Fr. Clem told me the story of the Good Shepherd, Who seeks out His lost sheep. Through this story and Fr. Clem's kindness, I felt I had a personal encounter with St. Francis. Ever since, I have deeply admired men and women who have answered God's call to enter religious life (though I eventually discerned that my vocation was elsewhere).

I thank God that I grew up in a loving Catholic family. The five of us—my mom Pat, my dad Harold, my younger sister Teresa, and my little brother Brian—kept the Faith at the heart of our lives. My dad was treasurer of the parish council; my mom was an active member of the women's club. When I wasn't singing in the youth choir, I served as a lector, along with Teresa.

Both within and outside our parish, we had a close community. We lived in the Midwest, on the lakeshore of western Michigan. We had plenty of school, neighborhood, and family activities to keep us busy, and if we ever got bored, we could just go visit our grandparents, aunts and uncles, cousins, and friends.

Our parents loved us deeply. Though Mom has been gone for more than twenty years, I vividly remember how joyful she was. She went out of her way to make everyone feel special, even strangers, and she always took care to dress nicely, especially for Mass. She had such a devotion to her Faith, to Mary, to the sacraments, and to our family. Mom filled our home with symbols of our Faith, including beautiful framed images of the Sacred Heart of Jesus and the Immaculate Heart of Mary. Through Mom's love, we came to know the love of God.

Our parents wanted only the best for us, but as Teresa, Brian, and I grew up, we started challenging Mom and Dad's ideas about what we should and shouldn't do. The three of us went to a Catholic high school known for its partying scene. Alcohol flowed at postgame house parties. Eventually, peer pressure cracked my resolve to stay away, and I discovered how much fun could be had after just a few drinks. My fear of consequences, though, mostly kept me in check. Certainly, I was attracted to sinful things, and I enjoyed the thrill of rebellion; nevertheless, I didn't want to ruin my life, and so I took care to maintain my grades and my reputation.

As careful as I was about my own actions, I couldn't keep my siblings from breaking our parents' hearts. Teresa fell in love with Tim, the boy next door. At sixteen, she became pregnant. I will never forget my mom's cry when she heard the news. Yet despite their shock and disappointment, Mom and Dad loved my sister dearly, and they were overjoyed when their first grand-child, a girl, was born. Tim became Catholic and married Teresa. After twenty years, their marriage ended in divorce — another tremendous heartbreak.

Brian, too, distressed my parents by having a child out of wedlock. His girlfriend already had two children when she be-came pregnant with his. After telling our parents the news, Brian married his girlfriend at the courthouse. Mom tried so hard to accept and love her daughter-in-law, but she worried about what the marriage would do to Brian. Meanwhile, I was thrilled to be a cool aunt to my nieces and nephews. I showered them with love and attention.

No matter what we did, we could always be certain of Mom's love. We were devastated when, at age fifty-nine, she died sud-denly from a heart attack. Though she was alone when she passed away, we all had a chance to say goodbye. Dad, her last visitor, brought her a root beer float. She died in her sleep on a Sunday night, at peace, holding her blue rosary. Four days later, we held her funeral Mass, which was said by not one but two priests. So many people came to pour out their love for Mom.

I kept thinking about all the advice she gave us: say your prayers, don't skip Confession, go to Our Lady, stay strong in your Faith. Oh, and: "Mary Loretta, you should wear more comfort-able shoes." Everyone needs that kind of guidance, and without it, we were reeling with grief. To whom could we turn?

The four of us went in different directions. Dad became ro-mantically involved with other ladies (yes, they were Catholic). He told me he was done being a parent; now he just wanted to be a friend to us kids. With no one to guide them, Teresa and Brian continued to struggle with their family problems. Alone and numb, I took a job six hours away in Indianapolis, and I resolved to remain steadfast in my Faith, come what may. Our Lord and Our Lady took care of me. It was no accident that the perfect apartment in my new city was right next to a Catholic church. I was far from home, without my mom at my side, but I realized that the Holy Family would be with me wherever I went.

That was all twenty years ago. Life has continued to take us down our various paths. I'm now married to my loving husband Michael, with whom I've worked hard to build a comfortable, faith-filled life. Mostly, I'm happy. But heartbreakingly, I can't say the same for my brother and sister.

Once active in her church, Teresa fell away from the Faith after she and Tim divorced. In her despair, she attempted suicide. I spent many sleepless nights praying for her recovery. Slowly, she healed. She moved in with her boyfriend, himself an ex-Catholic divorcé. Teresa's daughter, my niece Meg, is now married. She hasn't baptized her little boy, having traded her Catholic Faith for New Age beliefs. I've encouraged Teresa and Meg to turn to God for comfort, but to no avail.

Brian divorced his first wife and, after a few months of dating, married a woman with three ex-husbands. Brian had three children with his first wife, as well as two stepchildren, whom he raised as his own. None of the babies were baptized. Everything is a struggle for my brother. He has had many girlfriends over the years and just can't seem to find what he is looking for.

I make monthly trips up to Michigan to visit my family. I used to break down crying all the time on my way back to Indiana. I was so angry with my brother and sister and so overcome with worry for their souls. I kept thinking about how disgusted I was with how they'd chosen to live. I just disliked them so much. Eventually, I became confrontational with my siblings. I didn't give a thought to charity or kindness or patience. I just let them have it, which was the worst thing I could have done.

It was during one of these trips that I discovered EWTN radio. I happened to be driving along the stretch of US 31 called the St. Joseph Parkway, which is special to me because St. Joseph is one of my favorite saints. EWTN became a significant part of my road trips. The hosts and callers alike just seemed to get it! I especially enjoyed listening to Jerry and Debbie, and I wound up downloading the EWTN app so I could tune in every day.

Now, around this time, I started feeling my conscience nagging me to go to Confession. I'd started going to Mass twice a week, but I hadn't been to Confession in several years. Anxiety made me put it off until one day, out of the blue, Jerry and Debbie spent their entire show talking about Confession! I realized how much God wanted me to return to Him, and so I resolved to go to a Lenten penance service the week before Holy Week.

The lines were long that night, even with ten priests hearing Confessions. Nervously, I wondered which priest to pick. I didn't want to confess to a priest I knew well, which ruled out almost every priest at the parish (and even in the diocese!). Eventually, I joined the line for the oldest priest there. He was about ninety years old and reminded me of my dear Fr. Clem, the Franciscan who had won my heart for God that night in my grandpa's car.

Heart thumping, I reviewed the examination of conscience I'd pulled up on my iPhone.

"These people must think I'm on Facebook or something," I thought, looking out of the corner of my eye at the parishioners standing beside me. "I sure hope not."

At last, my turn came. I walked inside, shut the door, took a deep breath, and sat down directly in front of the priest. I wanted to make my Confession face to face.

"Bless me, Father, for I have sinned," I began. "It has been several years since my last Confession."

Then, I told him everything: how much I resented Teresa and Brian for leaving the Faith, how angry their wild habits made me, how unkind I was to them. All my bitter grief welled up, no longer buried and hidden inside, but poured out and offered to Christ. Anxious and weary though I was, I could feel His love filling my heart and comforting me.

When I had finished, the priest made a gentle joke about my long absence from the confessional, and then he said, "I can tell you love your family. But you must learn to love them with the love of Christ. That means not criticizing them, but being Christ to them. That's how you share His love with others."

From that moment on, through God's grace, I treated my siblings differently. I stopped lecturing them; instead, I began listening to their woes, showing interest in their lives, and offering words of encouragement. I decided to go out of my way to perform little acts of kindness and love, just as my mom did, so that my family could know how deeply I love them. I still struggle with not coming down on them for their sinful ways, but I now ask the Holy Spirit to guide me to a more loving approach. I came to understand that my duty is to live my Faith and let everyone see Christ in me.

I used to be ashamed and embarrassed to offer prayer intentions, but now I never miss an opportunity to offer up my family to the Lord, though they may never realize how much I pray for them. I offer each decade of my daily Rosary for a different member of my family. I offer special prayers, especially the powerful Memorare, for those who have upset me the most. I say morning prayers of intercession; I pray ongoing novenas to Mary, Undoer of Knots; I repeat "Jesus, I trust in You" throughout the day. St.

Monica and St. Padre Pio are my close friends, and St. Teresa of Calcutta is my new Oprah, my endless inspiration. Our Lord is always with me, and Our Blessed Lady holds my hand whenever I ask her to. They send me signs of love out of the blue when I'm at my lowest. As Jerry Usher says, "Take a couple of steps closer to God, and He will take a hundred steps closer to you!"

To put my own spin on it: take a couple of steps closer to God, surrender just a little to Him, and He will work miracles. God has shown me small glimmers of light in my family's hearts. My nieces and nephews always respond to my messages, whereas they used to ignore me. Teresa is kinder. I've seen her wearing the Miraculous Medal I gave her. I finally convinced Dad to receive Communion at Sunday Mass as often as he can. From Jerry and Debbie, I learned that we should devote ourselves to the Eucharist because we can offer up the graces of Holy Communion for our loved ones, especially those who have caused us the greatest heartache.

I don't know what the future holds, but I will continue to trust. Thank you, Jerry and Debbie, for your "friendship in the car." You have no idea how much you've meant to me.

"When Are You Going to Make Your Confession?"

By Carol Burdett

∞

I've always known that God works in mysterious ways. I knew that He would answer the prayer I said every morning for forty years: "Please, Lord, keep my husband here on earth until he comes to know and love You as I do, so that one day we'll be together with You for eternity." But I could never have predicted just how God brought Bob home.

Let me tell you a bit about my husband and our marriage. We married young: I was in my late teens. Bob was Catholic because his mother was. My parents gave me no religious instruction. They thought I should be free to choose my own religion. I discovered Christianity and encountered Jesus when I was sixteen. During my engagement to Bob, I felt a strong desire to become Catholic, and I converted in my eighteenth year.

I could sense that Bob was searching for the Lord but not finding the answers he wanted. He never said so explicitly; he didn't like talking about feelings or faith. We loved each other, and it broke my heart when, busy with his work as a car salesman, Bob stopped attending Mass with our family. He would join us for Baptisms and Confirmations, but that was it.

Looking back now, I can see signs that the Holy Spirit was moving in my husband. Some of His inspirations were small, as when He moved Bob to start reading the Bible every now and then. Others were sudden, enormous changes of heart. Once a functional alcoholic, Bob simply quit drinking for good one day. For so many years, he'd "needed to keep a buzz on," as he put it, but he was sober for the last twenty-eight years of our marriage.

The second significant change was even grander than the first. At the time, I was working for the Post Office as a rural mail carrier, and Bob was working from home as a real-estate broker. His days off were very flexible, and I'd saved up quite a bit of vacation time. So when Bob found a great deal on a fifteen-day repositioning cruise from Portugal to Galveston, Texas, we were quick to book our tickets and arrange travel with our friends Pat and Jerry.

Since we had to fly overseas anyway, we decided to begin our trip in Paris. We stayed in a sixteenth-century hotel within walking distance of Notre Dame. Every day, Mass was celebrated in a small chapel in front of Nicolas Coustou's beautiful *Pietà*. All four of us, even Bob, attended. Even though we didn't know French, the Mass was familiar, and its beauty touched our hearts — especially Bob's, I suspect. After four days in Paris and another in Portugal, we boarded our ship home.

Since Jerry and I were early risers, unlike our spouses, we met on the deck for coffee before Pat and Bob joined us for breakfast. The first morning at sea, when I went to the café for coffee, there sat Jerry conversing with another man.

"Guess who this is?" Jerry asked as I approached. "Meet Fr. Dale. He'll be celebrating daily Mass for us!"

Fr. Dale stood up and shook my hand.

"Hi, Carol," he said. "It's nice to meet you. Jerry was just saying that you lector at Mass back home — would you be able to do the readings this morning?"

Unaware that the day's readings contained a slew of compli-cated names, I agreed. Boy, was I embarrassed when I stepped down from the lectern: I'd thoroughly butchered every one of those unfamiliar words.

"You'll probably never ask me to do that again," I told Fr. Dale afterward.

"Oh, no," he assured me, "none of us can pronounce them either. Could you do the readings every morning while we're here?"

That was how we established our little routine for Mass. Every day, we met in the lounge area by the bar, which was the only place with enough room for Mass. Here, we had no stark kneelers, but heavy mahogany tables and comfortable leather chairs. I did the readings; when needed, Jerry and Pat helped Fr. Dale distribute Communion. Bob came to Mass with us, though he did not join us in the Communion line. Once Mass had ended, the five of us headed to the dining area for a mouth-watering breakfast.

Fr. Dale was delightful company. We got to know him well, since he always seemed to know just where we spent our on-deck time. We went almost everywhere together. Yet Fr. Dale was working under the radar, as we soon discovered.

One morning, when Jerry, Pat, and I returned to our table after Communion, we were surprised to see that Bob wasn't there waiting for us. Jerry looked over his shoulder and then silently motioned for us to look at the Communion line. And there was the scene I'd been waiting to see for forty years: my husband, hands folded and head bowed, in line to receive Jesus. I couldn't believe it.

Bob said nothing when he returned. An hour later, while I was still in tearful shock, Fr. Dale joined us for breakfast. He thumbed his suspenders and grinned.

"You were surprised, weren't you?" he asked. "And I didn't give it away during coffee, did I?"

∞

It came out that Fr. Dale had directly asked Bob when he planned on coming back to the Church. Bob kept saying it wasn't going to happen, but Fr. Dale persisted.

"When are you going to make your Confession so you can get back to Communion?" he asked over and over.

Now, I should mention that Fr. Dale had spent some years as a Marine chaplain. He neither gave up easily nor accepted wishy-washy answers. I don't know exactly what he said to convince Bob, but it didn't matter. There he was, back in communion with his Church.

Overjoyed as I was, I remained skeptical. It seemed unlikely that Bob would fully embrace his long-lost Faith, and so I adopted a wait-and-see attitude toward his conversion. But when we returned home and Saturday evening came, there he was. He never skipped Mass again. Instead, he would drop me off at choir practice and return from shopping in time to join the little group of new friends whom he sat with at every vigil Mass. He took over saying grace before meals, even when we were out with friends. He was more relaxed than I could ever remember.

I'd asked God to keep Bob on earth long enough for him to return to the Faith, so that we could spend eternity together. Not only did God bring Bob back into a state of grace, but He gave us six more years together in this life, before He called Bob home.

Even in the accident that caused Bob's death, I could see how God lovingly cared for us. We'd survived an awful tornado that stripped six hundred trees from our home grounds. Our house, our pets, and our horses all escaped without serious damage. Within a year, we were able to get the areas around our house cleaned, cleared, and seeded into lawn. We found that we still had trees, ones that were small enough to bend with the wind and not be uprooted.

For years, we continued clearing the damaged trees. As Bob cut down a dead tree, I watched the top. The saw's vibrations could make the whole top break off and come crashing down. If I yelled anything, anything at all, Bob was to move.

One day, three years after the tornado, Bob was cutting down three trees so I could build a fire and burn an unsightly stump by our house. The first two trees came down smoothly, and it appeared that the third would follow suit, since it was already leaning. But somehow, it got caught on a cluster of nearby trees, and when Bob went to finish putting it on the ground, it slid down silently until it fell right on top of him.

The next few minutes were surreal. The saw was still running: in my panic, I couldn't find the kill switch. I wound up tossing the saw out of the way, so I could feel for Bob's pulse. He was breathing, and as I ran to the house to call 911, I prayed, "Keep him breathing, Lord. Breathe for him."

One of the area EMTs happened to be driving near our house on his way home when the call came, and he diverted immediately to help. Bob was airlifted to the University of Tennessee trauma hospital—another sign God was there, watching over us. For many reasons, I hadn't wanted him to go to the local hospital.

Our daughter Kathy, who lived nearby, drove me to Knoxville, where her husband was already with Bob. Our oldest son and youngest daughter lived many states away, but they were on their way. Our youngest child lived two hours from the hospital and met us there, along with Bob's sisters and some of our friends.

God bless the medical staff at the hospital. They did everything they could, even restarting Bob's heart twice, but there was no hope. Bob hung on long enough for a Catholic priest to administer last rites, and then we had to let him go. I know he lives on, not only in the next life, but also here on earth, in a way: as was always his wish, Bob's organs were donated after he died. We received a wonderful medal to commemorate his act of charity.

It's been ten years now since Bob died. What have I learned from our life together? We serve a mighty God, Who always answers our prayers. In the end, I just had to be patient and let God work. Too often, in our haste to make life turn out all right, we grab at every possible opportunity to fix things. I know I did. But I wasn't the one who finally brought my husband home: it was Our Lord, through Fr. Dale.

I wonder if Fr. Dale was one of God's angels on earth. He was unobtrusively focused on Bob and nonchalant about blending into our little group. He was simply there, offering good company, sharing the famed cruise meals and the books we were reading. He was the right person at the right time with the right words.

Fr. Dale wasn't the only priest we met who might have been an angel. The priest at the hospital who gave Bob last rites was amazingly easy to find on such short notice, especially since he spoke little English and all the priests in the diocese were away on retreat. Our own pastor, Fr. Jim, was on that retreat, counties away. But he was at our side the next day to plan Bob's celebration of life, and he helped us grieve during and after the beautiful service a few days later.

I wish Bob could be here to finish this story and to explain the peace he experienced when he returned to the Church. What lessons would he share from his years away? What wonderful stories will he have of his new life with Our Lord?

All I know is that he's at peace forever. And I'm at peace too.

You and One Left Shoe

By Penny Stout

I was raised in a small, predominantly Baptist town. With the exception of my maternal grandmother, my family was abusive and neglectful. My dad had drug and anger issues; my mom was mentally ill. My half-brother abused us until he finally moved out. When I was ten, my dad left to be with his girlfriend, and we no longer had contact with his side of the family. Then, five years later, my mom decided my sister and I were old enough to care for ourselves. She didn't want to be a parent anymore.

Growing up, I attended youth groups and church functions sporadically. I was baptized in my early teens. Although my faith was always strong, I never felt convicted to attend church; in fact, I didn't have much use for organized religion. When I married my husband, Nick, I jumped through all the Catholic hoops for him. But I had no respect for the institution of marriage. For me, divorce wasn't an "if," but a "when."

Predictably, my marriage was in shambles within a year. I had an affair. I told Nick I wanted a divorce. After Nick found out what I had done, he didn't scream at me or call me names, though I felt he was entitled to. Instead, he simply sat down with me and apologized for however he had contributed to my decision to have an affair.

"I still choose you," Nick said. "I still want to be married to you."

I have never known such love or forgiveness in my entire life. This was a pivotal moment for me. My entire life, I sat on a pedestal of superiority, secure in the fact that I was a good person who didn't do bad things. And then I made the biggest mistake of my life. I never expected Nick would want to stay together. Divorce was the legacy of my family. When things got hard, all the married couples I knew quit. Divorce would have been easy; staying together was the hardest thing we have ever done.

Nick and I attended counseling. We picked up a dusty book called *Love and Respect* from the shelf and read it together. We "moved forward," as they say, but I never felt as if the issue were resolved. I felt a stain on my soul, and I had no idea how to fix it. When I jumped through those Catholic hoops, I hadn't realized that our marriage bond was indissoluble. Neither of us could just get a civil divorce and move on. Our marriage actually meant something to Nick. So did his Faith.

That was my first glimpse of the amazing man I married. I truly believe that every blessing in my life stems from this period of hardship, when I learned from my husband what it meant to be a Christian.

At this point, my in-laws were justifiably upset. From the beginning, they'd had concerns about our compatibility. Clearly, we were unequally yoked. But Nick was their oldest child, and they wanted to handle the situation with sensitivity.

Nick's friendships, or lack thereof, concerned his parents. They didn't think it was appropriate for a married person to have single friends. We would defiantly say that we picked our friends based on who they were, not on their relationship status.

It seemed wrong to think that we couldn't trust each other around our unmarried friends.

Around this time, I met my best friend, Rachel. She made me feel normal again. I would openly discuss my affair with her, and I was able to talk to her about how I felt I had damaged my soul. Within a few years, Rachel moved in with us. She was having problems with her parents. We had a large home, and she paid rent. We made our own family and limited contact with Nick's family.

My upbringing kept me from wanting to have children. I had an overwhelming fear that I would fail my children just as my parents had failed me. But Nick's grandfather—a practicing Catholic—prayed constantly that God would move my heart to accept children as a blessing. That man was my spiritual compass. Though I told him I would never convert to Catholicism, he loved and prayed for me all the same. He bought me the most beautiful rosary for my wedding bouquet. He was yet another example for me of Christian love and kindness.

When Nick and I finally opened our hearts to the possibility of starting a family, I became pregnant almost immediately. It was during my pregnancy that I started listening to EWTN. Nick had left the radio set to the station, and from then on, I secretly listened to it in the car. As my baby shifted and kicked and fluttered in my womb, I would listen to people on the radio talking about the atrocities committed by Planned Parenthood. My opinions on abortion and a woman's right to choose began to change. Under the guise of learning about Nick's religion, I kept tuning in to EWTN. The truth was that it was the only place where I could find hope amidst the Planned Parenthood scandals and the presidential election that was underway. And I had fallen in love with a nun named Mother Angelica. We had the same favorite color: yellow. She was the first to teach me that we can offer our suffering and pain to God.

∞

Becoming a mother was another turning point in my faith story. Shortly after our daughter Mara was born, a storm blew in and the power went out. I was in the nursery rocking Mara, trying to be brave. I remember worrying about the storm and my baby's temperature and her weight, and then for no reason at all, I started thinking about Mother Mary. As I sat there holding my baby, I thought about Mary doing the same for Jesus. I was humbled. Having been raised a Baptist, I'd always thought of Mary as a vessel for the Incarnation, nothing more. She was irrelevant. Without a loving mother figure, I'd never imagined what Mary must have experienced. Now I can think of little else.

I once saw this movie where a lady buys a house. The previous owners left behind a bed with a beautiful painting of the Virgin Mary over it. One night, the woman rides out an awful storm clinging to the headboard and looking at Mary. The character in the movie wasn't Catholic, but she talked about how Mary became like her favorite aunt. That's what happened to me as well.

I also began to think about Nick's mother. I owed her an apology for the strife I caused in her family. I needed her advice and guidance. She was a good mother to all of her children, and I had treated her with disrespect. I slowly began to reach out to her and tried to mend our relationship.

After Mara was born, we sold our home, which I owned prior to our marriage, to purchase property in a small community closer to Nick's family. We planned to build our home, but after very disorganized and sporadic communication, we received notice that the builder had filed for bankruptcy. We lost a large portion of our build budget and were in shock. During this time, I knew in my heart that God had decided not to allow our project to move forward. We always say "God's will be done," but this was the first time that I chose to lean on my faith instead of wallowing in anger and despair. Rachel, Nick, and I moved into an apartment and then, eventually, into the home Rachel inherited from her grandfather.

Rachel was frustrated with the church that her family had helped to found. She told us that she was going to convert to Catholicism. I honestly wasn't surprised by her decision: she had attended a Catholic school, and during the previous presidential election, I had encouraged her to listen to EWTN, which was one of the only places we could go for inspirational, uplifting messages instead of doom and gloom. Rachel and I began having intense discussions about everything that was happening, and I knew how disillusioned she had become. So I told her I would happily attend RCIA with her, but I was not going to convert.

I held firm in my resolve until the day of Nick's grandfather's funeral. As I stood surrounded by all of his children, grandchildren, and their families, I realized what an immense hole he'd left in our hearts. He had done so much good for us all. We were all just selfishly sad to see him go, even though we knew, given the life he led, that he was with God.

I decided right then that I was going to convert and raise my child in the Church.

∞

When Nick's grandfather talked to me about converting, I always responded with my list of dealbreakers. The saints were idols.

Catholics had a weird obsession with Mary. Purgatory sounded like a bunch of hooey, and Confession was a ridiculous concept because I talked directly to God, thank you very much. Through RCIA and EWTN, I came to see the truth about all these issues. I needed the Church to guide me and the daughter God had entrusted to me.

Rachel and I became Catholic, and she became Mara's godmother. It was a lovely event for everyone. I remember feeling I was finally on the right track to become the person God intended me to be.

Three days before my ten-year wedding anniversary, I found a letter Rachel had written to Nick. In it, I read that they had been having an affair for a long time, and that Rachel hated me. The two people I cared about the most had been living in this sin for so long.

I was crushed. I begged them to go to Confession. Then, I told Nick he had to choose either me or Rachel. He was in shock that I actually expected him to make a decision; she was livid that he didn't immediately choose her.

Quickly, I packed a bag for Mara and called my older sister. I spent that night with a friend. I was in total shock; my entire world had been turned upside down.

The next morning, I woke up to Mara's angelic face. She had no idea that her world had just changed forever. As I got us both ready for the day, I realized I had packed everything she needed, and the only thing I had grabbed for myself was one left shoe. That day, a new saying came into my life: you and one left shoe. It became my mantra. I had just walked away from everything I owned, with no clue how we would survive, but I knew we would figure it out, because I had my daughter and one left shoe. Later, I saw this saying in light of my faith. If God was with me, nothing else mattered.

Nick and I signed a six-month lease on an apartment together to give us time to figure things out. We decided to seek intensive individual and couples counseling. It was important to me to seek out Christian counselors who would understand and respect the sacrament of Matrimony. This turned out to be one of the most crucial decisions that we made.

Nick promised a priest, his father, and me that he would have no contact with Rachel, but soon, I realized that Nick didn't even seem to know right from wrong anymore. Their relationship was on-again, off-again for some time. She continued to contact him regularly from multiple phone numbers, as well as coming to our apartment and his workplace. Rachel encouraged Nick to meet with a divorce lawyer, and she tried to convince our friends that I was an unfit mother, a manipulator, a narcissist, and so on. My doctor placed me on medication for panic attacks, and I knew that as much as I wanted to save our marriage, I couldn't do it alone. This situation was unsustainable.

After one particularly painful counseling session, I blew up and threw a challenge out to Nick. I told him just to go to Rachel. All darkness would come to light. When everything became public knowledge, no longer masked by the fog of sin, and he had to look himself and others in the face, this sin wouldn't be fun anymore.

I never expected him not to come home that night. I went through the motions: I made dinner, brushed Mara's teeth, and tucked her into bed. I called him and begged him to come home. In all my life, I have never felt as devastated as I did that lonely night. In the morning, all I felt was a dull, dry ache in my soul. I stood in front of the mirror crying and begging myself to hold on and be strong. When I think back on this time in my life, I visualize the people you see in Pompeii. I felt like I was made of ash. One strong breeze and I would be scattered.

In my rawness, I didn't want to see anyone but my in-laws and my sister, because they were the only people I knew who loved my daughter as much as I did. My in-laws came to be with me early that morning, and they comforted me. They allowed me time to mourn and then insisted that I start making plans for my future, with or without their son. I cannot imagine how hard it was for them to stand beside me during this time. They were disappointed in Nick and scared for Mara, but they still had to speak truth to me, no matter how painful it was. Nick was convinced that his family had chosen me over him, but as painful as it was, they had chosen right over wrong.

That night was a turning point for me. It was upsetting to acknowledge that I had placed my daughter in the very situation in which I'd grown up. Would her father, like mine, leave for good to be with another woman? Would we matter to Nick once he moved on? I was stuck between giving up and wondering "What if?" I wished I could change the past, but I soon realized that there is a reason the rearview mirror is so small and the windshield is so big. We don't need to look back, because we aren't going that way.

It was a struggle just to get to the next day. Some days, life seemed a grand adventure, but other days were an uncomfortable necessity before sleep. I've heard that it's not the person you miss, but the routine. Without Nick, my routine had become torture. My therapist told me, "Depression is when you don't care about anything; anxiety is when you care too much about everything. Having both is a living hell."

I started to overthink more and more. I could feel myself pulling away from everyone, not just Nick. I knew he and I needed to communicate, to heal, to get everything out, but I was scared to say the things that needed to be said. I really didn't want to hurt him. What if I pushed him away? And yet how could I look at Mara someday and tell her I stopped fighting for her future? He hadn't just left me: he left us. That was the one thing I couldn't seem to get over. But I didn't want to stay married "for our daughter's sake." How could either of us want her to grow up in this kind of family?

During this time, while Nick was so set on finding faults in me, I was too busy overlooking his. The standards I had set for us didn't seem to mean anything anymore. He wasn't afraid of losing me because he knew I would always be willing to give him one more chance. I had planned my life and created my identity around Nick. We'd been together since we were twenty. Everything I was so proud of turned out to be a lie. I desperately wanted a plan for our future, or even just some hint from him that we were moving forward together, but his insistence that we take it one day at a time finally forced me to start looking inside myself. I decided I didn't want to become comfortable with disrespect. Whatever I allowed would continue.

The best thing about the worst time in your life is that you get to see everyone's true colors, including your own. I couldn't control what was happening, so I decided to take control of the only thing I could: my reaction. There comes a point when the damage is too much, and no matter how good things used to be, the memories can't sustain you. Especially when all your memories are clouded by lies. Closure happens right after you accept that letting go and moving on are more important than fantasizing about how the relationship could have been. I didn't want to push Nick away, but if he was going to choose Rachel, all I could do was control my reaction. I am sorry to say that my childhood made me quite good at letting people go.

I began to say the Rosary on a regular basis, using the same rosary that Nick's grandfather had given me for my wedding bouquet. Through repetitive prayer, I started to feel calm. My faith started to blossom. As much as I was tired of fighting, I knew I had to keep trying. God didn't tell me to move the stone; He just told me to push. As I fought, God tirelessly sent me signs of His support and love. One day, when I was listening to EWTN, the presenter happened to mention Romans 8:18. I went to look up the verse, which said, "I consider that the sufferings of this present time are as nothing compared with the glory to be revealed to us." All I could think was that Nick and I were married on August 18 — 8/18. This beautiful message from God got me through so many hard days.

One night, Nick was planning to get dinner and come over. My cousin was in town, and I was looking forward to a quiet night. Then, I got a text from Nick telling me that he was at Rachel's house, he didn't love me, and he would never end his relationship with her. In tears, I called my father-in-law and begged him to tell me what to do. He was so calm and kind. He told me that Nick didn't respect me and that I couldn't keep holding our marriage together. In that moment, I truly believe the Holy Spirit was with me. I realized that if Nick intended to be with Rachel, she would be a part of our lives, whether I liked it or not, and I couldn't ignore her anymore. I hung up the phone, asked my cousin to watch Mara, and calmly drove to Rachel's house.

When I arrived, the front door was open, and I walked in. Nick came downstairs in a panic. He told me that Rachel had taken his phone. He didn't know what she had sent me.

Rachel came downstairs screaming, cussing, and spewing the vilest things. From the look on Nick's face, I could tell that he was shocked not only by how she was acting, but also by what she was saying. For the first time, he got to see the damage he had done to all of us.

For a few moments, I lashed out at Rachel, but the longer I looked at her, the more I saw her — really saw her. She was pale and thin. She was in so much pain, and she was scared. Looking at her, I remembered the person who was my friend. Not everything could have been a lie. She was still a beloved child of God. I felt a wave of forgiveness and compassion for her.

I knew at that moment that Nick would leave with me and our marriage would survive. When Rachel saw the shift in him, she was crushed. She crumpled to the ground, and I ended up holding her, kneeling in the hallway, and praying with and for her. She pleaded to stay friends; she begged to see Mara again, and she was desperately clawing at any opportunity to stay connected. I knew I couldn't allow any of this. But I also knew I was no longer angry with her. I had forgiven her, and I truly wanted her to be okay.

It didn't all end right then; there was no clean break, but Nick and I have discussed that night multiple times, and surreal as it seemed, it was the turning point for us. I always thought that every story had a villain and that the villain in our story was surely Rachel. But she wasn't a villain any more than Nick or I was. We all made terrible mistakes. We ignored sound Christian advice because it wasn't convenient, and we all paid a terrible price for it.

Mistakes have so much power. They will turn you into something better than you were before. Sometimes, it's not about having strength to hold on, but having the courage to let go. Forgive yourself and others. Stop replaying negative situations over and over. Don't hold yourself hostage to your past mistakes or remind yourself of what should have been. Monsters don't hide under beds; they creep around in your head.

I told Nick that he had to start slow, with just one right choice. Just make one choice, and then build on it, until one day, he could look up and be proud of himself.

We started building our marriage back up from rock bottom—good, solid ground on which to lay a foundation. Just because we have made mistakes in our marriage does not mean that our marriage is a mistake. When the Japanese mend a broken object, they fill the cracks with gold. Its flaws become beautiful and only increase the object's value. This is how I view my marriage. God has filled every crack and smoothed every ragged edge with His grace and love. My broken marriage is now beautiful and strong because it was damaged and then repaired.

As we built our marriage back up, Nick and I finished building the home that we started five years ago. I wrote Scripture on the studs of the house, making sure to include Jeremiah 29:11: "For I know well the plans I have in mind for you ... plans for your welfare and not for woe, so as to give you a future of hope."

Looking back on this entire journey, I am so thankful that God intervened to keep us from building our home any sooner. We may have had a building in which to live, but the foundation of our marriage would have remained on sand. God doesn't say no. When He doesn't say yes, it's because He has something better in mind. Time and again, this has been the case in my life. Nick and I are expecting our second daughter this year. She would never have existed if we hadn't fought to save our marriage.

In my mind, love is no longer this childish thing involving chocolate roses and candy hearts. Our marriage is not a

Hallmark movie. Love is damaged and hard-won. It's something precious, but not fragile, something that has been nailed to a cross and made holy. Spouses must suffer together. Yet they shouldn't suffer needlessly because of each other. Never cause your spouse pain, and take second chances seriously. Most importantly, don't give yourself the opportunity to fall in love with someone else. God will never send you someone else's husband or wife. If you think you have married the wrong person, look at your marriage certificate. If you have been validly married in the Church, the person named there is the one you are meant to be with.

Finding Faith in a Changing Church

By Bernadette James

◇◇◇

My five younger siblings and I grew up in a midsize city in the Midwest. Our parents, who met in college, grew up regularly attending Sunday Mass. They were taught that God is good, no question about it. My mom's parents were active in their parish community: Grandpa was a regular usher, and Grandma was in-volved in the Altar and Rosary Society. She would typically make items for the bake sale, bring them to the church, and then buy them so she could take them home again. All their friends were Catholic, and they all attended events together at the church.

My upbringing involved a lot of moving around from school to school as my parents tried to find the best one for us kids. Unfortunately, my parents kept discovering that many of these schools were less than ideal. My second-grade teacher, a religious sister, was not well suited to teach young children: she screamed at me when I accidentally broke the teacup saucer my mom had given me for an art project. This incident helped my mom determine that this school wasn't the best place for me, though she didn't remove me right away, and I finished out the school year with this teacher.

My parents tried public school, then Catholic school, and then public school again. Finally, they settled on a small suburban K–6 school run by a no-nonsense Irish priest and an order of Irish sisters, still in full habits. The priest explained that the school had no set tuition fee; instead, families contributed what they could to the Sunday offertory for their tuition. Such a system would be almost unheard-of today. My dad joined the board and became a lector at the parish.

The first four of us kids graduated from this little school. Then, it was back to public school. I went back and forth between two school districts, until I graduated from high school in a class of over nine hundred students. In a similar way, my siblings bounced around between different public and private schools.

My parents did their best to give us a good Catholic education, but the Second Vatican Council had caused the Church to change quickly in the late sixties and seventies. As my mom told me years later, when I was an adult, she was mad that the Church of her youth had disappeared. She was very busy raising the six of us and didn't have the time to discover for herself what Vatican II really taught. My parents grew up in an era when no one questioned authority. When all these changes came along, my parents didn't question the Church hierarchy; instead, they got angry and blamed the changes on Vatican II.

Looking back, I can see how some of these changes kept me from fully understanding and practicing my Faith. For example, churches began to adopt a folksy, casual approach to the liturgy at the expense of reverence. When I was little, the only instrument used at Mass was the organ, and nuns almost always wore habits. But as I grew up, our neighborhood parish began to introduce other instruments, and the nuns took to wearing fashionable secular clothes. I'll never forget the time I saw a nun at our church wearing a miniskirt.

The most significant consequence of this laid-back approach was the loss of reverence toward the Eucharist, especially once Communion rails were removed and communicants were allowed to receive the Eucharist in the hand. I think this is why most American Catholics today don't know—or don't accept—what the Church teaches about the Real Presence. The disappearance of sacramental preparation during that time didn't help either. I made my First Communion in the second grade, but at the time, there was no mention of First Reconciliation. Fast forward to fifth grade, when my entire class was going to Confession one day. Our teacher, Sr. Maria, saw that I had not gotten in line. She didn't ask what was wrong, but simply told me to line up with everyone else.

As far as I can remember, that was my First Reconciliation. I was unprepared; I didn't know what to say and, in fact, probably thought I had nothing to confess.

As for Confirmation, all I remember is that the church was crowded, the bishop was progressive, and my brother Tony and I got to go to a special restaurant for dinner afterward—without having our younger siblings in tow. It's sad that going out to dinner left a bigger impression on me than receiving the sacrament did, but my experience is not uncommon among the folks of my generation. Most of us hardly remember receiving any kind of instruction on how to receive the sacraments, which were just another box to check off. Back then, there was so much emphasis placed on going through the motions that we didn't usually stop to think about what we were doing or why. It's no surprise, then, that none of us felt close to God. We didn't have a relationship with Him.

I later discovered that these new practices—loss of reverence in the liturgy, especially toward the Eucharist, and lack of sacramental preparation—were actually the opposite of what Vatican II intended. But as I mentioned, my parents didn't fully understand what happened at the Council, and so they couldn't explain why everything was changing. Like many Catholic children at the time, my siblings and I were left to figure things out for ourselves. As a result, we didn't learn how to respond to the secular world's many challenges to our Faith, and all five of my younger siblings changed their religious beliefs in some way once they reached their early twenties.

In college, my brother Tony became close friends with some Protestants. He learned to read Proverbs every day, but also developed a great disdain for Our Blessed Mother that continues to this day. Next in line is my sister Olivia, who began an immoral relationship in college. After fourteen years of "dating," she and her boyfriend got married in an outdoor ceremony, with a female minister presiding. They have adopted two boys from Africa. Then there's my brother Vito, who took a job in the movie industry, where immoral behavior was the norm. He and his wife were married in Grand Central Station by a licensed therapist who also witnessed marriages. They, too, adopted a girl from overseas, China in this case.

Sibling number four, Frank, married a Protestant young lady who converted to the Catholic Faith the year they got married. However, at that time, their parish's RCIA program was lacking. They baptized their first child but ended up leaving the Church. My sister-in-law grew up in a church with a nursery, and she didn't like having to get up during Mass when her daughter was fussy. They settled on the local nondenominational start-up church, from which another start-up church has since broken off.

Finally, my youngest brother, George, fell in with some diabolical coworkers who may have placed a curse on him. He has since gotten heavily involved with marijuana and other drugs and has become wary of organized religion. While he has managed to hold down a job, there is no joy in his life. He and his girlfriend of several years live together, and their relationship is very sad.

I, too, might have left the Faith, had I not met Fr. Conrad, who was the campus minister at my college. He offered weekly classes for students and non-students alike on the real teachings of Vatican II and, once it was released, the new Catechism. He held weekend retreats for men and women, which he wisely chose to keep separate, given the many temptations young people face. On retreat, he focused on providing opportunities for Mass, Confession, and adoration, and he would present helpful talks throughout the weekend. We were all amazed by the truly joyful, peaceful atmosphere Fr. Conrad created for us, both on retreat and on campus.

As you can see, the Lord was present in my life more than I ever realized at the time. It is only in hindsight that one can look back and see things with more clarity. It takes practice to recognize God's grace being poured out on us every day. Everything that was missing in the changing Church of my youth, especially clear instruction and thorough formation, God supplied for me through Fr. Conrad. He helped me discover the importance of staying close to the sacraments (especially Confession and the Holy Eucharist), praying the Rosary daily, and having a regular holy hour. These practices have made all the difference for me: they helped me make a habit of recognizing God's grace and presence, instead of going through the motions the way so many people did when I was growing up. Knowing that God is with me gives me the spiritual strength to remain faithful and strong during hardships, including my marriage. I thought I married someone who shared my Catholic Faith, but that turned out not to be the case. We ended up getting a divorce and an annulment. At the time, the whole process didn't feel like a blessing, but through it, God healed me. He also blessed me with three sons, whom I raised in the Faith.

Today, my best days are when I attend daily Mass, say my Rosary, and get to adoration. As Mother Angelica used to say, having "holy reminders," or sacramentals, in my home helps me keep my focus on God, even when daily responsibilities can distract me from the big picture. Another way I stay focused on Him is spiritual direction. Spiritual directors help us keep discernment in check and make sure that we are not being misled by the Evil One in disguise. Also — I can't say it enough — frequent Confession is so important. Without it, we can't have a strong relationship with God, and we will be blind to His guidance.

Had my siblings known all this, or had they heard someone like Fr. Conrad explain the teachings of Vatican II, they might have remained in the Church. I continue to pray that they will be open to God's guidance. The best way I can help them is offering sacrifices and tucking them into my Rosary as often as possible. I also have to meet them where they are. Instead of trying to tell my siblings and their families how much they misunderstand the Church, I need to show them the love of Jesus, letting my actions speak louder than my words. To do this, we have only to look to the saints as our guides. Just think about the great love they had for everyone they met. This is how we must treat each other.

I'll end with this advice: ask your guardian angel to work with the guardian angels of your loved ones. Remember, Jesus began the parable of the lost sheep with the words: "See that you do not despise one of these little ones; for I say to their angels in heaven always look upon the face of my heavenly Father" (Matt. 18:10). Few passages in Scripture are as comforting.

Life on the Edge

By Catherine Pillar

∞

My late husband, Stephen, was born in 1941 on the feast of Sts. Perpetua and Felicity to faithful Catholic parents. He was one of seven children (four boys and three girls). Stephen's mother was a collegiate librarian, and his father was a former Navy officer, an attorney, and later a district-court judge. Both parents modeled the rules and virtues they expected their children to live by. Stephen and his siblings were groomed to appreciate a sophisticated lifestyle, to pursue higher education, to love academics, and to become active citizens. Later, both of Stephen's grandmothers moved in with the family, acting as strong, ideal models in the Faith.

Catholic education, restricted television, music lessons, required reading, sports, regular Mass attendance, Eagle Scout activities, grace before meals, and praying the Most Holy Rosary every night following dinner were pillars in Stephen's formation. If any friends showed up at the front door during the nightly Rosary, they knew to come in, kneel down, and join in. You didn't leave the house before the family Rosary: no exceptions.

Stephen was all about pursuing excellence in his endeavors. One of his favorite sayings was, "If you are not living on the edge, you are taking up too much space!" Voracious reading nurtured his wide array of interests, both related and unrelated to his pursuits in life. The world of literature offered untold adventures for his ever-inquiring mind. Thus the springboard for his theories about the world, which began to collide with his childhood Faith.

As his family expected, Stephen was awarded a scholarship to a prestigious university. There, away from parental scrutiny, Stephen abandoned his spiritual foundation and made academics and sports the twin pillars of his life. Without a second thought, he explained away his Catholic formation. He stopped going to Mass. Subtly, the atheistic ways of the world lured him in. Though intelligent, charming, and witty, Stephen was a worldly man with a parched soul.

After undergrad, Stephen entered a renowned law school on the East Coast. While pursuing his legal degree, Stephen developed strong critical-thinking and problem-solving skills. He had many redeeming qualities — a high IQ, membership in Mensa, volunteer work on various boards, and the ability to think quickly on his feet — but a deep faith was not one of them. His spiritual growth was stunted. The following anecdote best captures his sparkling wit and lackluster spirituality: several years into his legal career, Stephen served on a board in our diocese — until he told our bishop during a meeting, "You have one of the finest minds of the thirteenth century!" Needless to say, he was abruptly fired.

The pressure of being a high-level trial attorney (his legal practice handled Supreme Court cases) meant Stephen's life was anything but serene. His first marriage failed, and his wife, a lapsed Catholic, sought solace in drinking and smoking. Despite numerous interventions, she neither returned to her Faith nor found sobriety and serenity until she succumbed to multisystem organ failure. I pray for her soul to this day.

Smoking, drinking, pursuing things of the flesh, and living in the fast lane took their toll on Stephen's physical and spiritual health too. At age forty, he suffered his first heart attack. That's when I met him: I was his cardiac rehab nurse.

Stephen called me an angel. He said he had never met anyone so kind, genuine, and compassionate. I remembered him fondly, but I didn't expect him to call me out of the blue four years later. God always has a plan!

After several years of dating, we were married in the Church. I am reminded of those infamous naïve words: "I think I can change him!" In a sense, God knew what Stephen needed and who would be instrumental in helping him forge a circuitous path to Heaven. But that didn't mean Stephen always knew what was best for his soul.

During the time we were married, not once did Stephen consent to attend Mass with me, except for weddings and funerals. He did attend a local non-Catholic church on Sundays — but only to sing in its prestigious choir. Singing was his therapy and stress-reliever of sorts, he said. Neither did he care about the mission of the church, nor did he pay attention to the preacher.

Stephen expressed both admiration and disgust for my ability to believe in what he could not explain or understand. A true lawyer, he never missed a chance to cross-examine me about why I could believe so easily and he could not at all.

"After all, between the two of us, I'm the one who's read the Bible cover to cover three times," he would say.

When he wasn't reading occult books out of curiosity, Stephen read intensely about all the failings of the Church and grilled me about the atrocities that priests had committed over the centuries. He spared no barbs when he heard me watching

EWTN on TV. He'd bully me and chastise me, demanding, "How can you believe any of that garbage?"

I couldn't understand how he could *not* believe. As I often told him, his head was only inches from his heart. He didn't have to keep the two so separate. But for an intellectual, especially one whose intelligence and curiosity had been weaponized by the Evil One, the distance between head and heart might as well have been a chasm.

And yet, through it all, my soul was not beaten down. Stephen did not intimidate me. God had given me the gift of faith in Him, a faith so strong and sure I could stake my life on it. This unshakeable confidence was my saving grace.

Deep down, Stephen must have recognized the power of my faith. Even as he put his soul at risk, walking close to the edge of Hell, he never once refused my prayers or blessings with holy water. But it wasn't until his second heart attack that he truly opened himself to God.

After two such crises, Stephen's heart was severely weakened. During open heart surgery, the doctors discovered that he had ischemic cardiomyopathy. As his condition progressed, they said, he would need a heart transplant.

The news jolted us both. To my horror, Stephen suggested that he would be better off dead than a cripple, especially because he would be a burden on me.

"Absolutely not," I said. "We're staying together, for better or for worse. That's what we promised. No turning back. It's in God's hands now."

I prayed unceasingly during the six months Stephen was in the hospital waiting for a donor heart. The plea that I had made every day of our marriage—"God, don't take Stephen until his soul is right with you"—became even more fervent. I didn't know how much time he had left. So I prayed in the elevator; I prayed at work; I prayed while driving. Every week, I called six priest friends to ensure they would pray for Stephen at each of their weekend Masses. Every free moment became an occasion for prayer.

As before, Stephen accepted my prayers without protest. In fact, he often told me to "keep rolling those beads" when he saw me praying the Rosary. At his bedside were stacks of cards from our friends, whose messages of hope and faith kept Stephen's spirits up. Again and again, he turned over five little words in his mind: "You are being prayed for."

Our prayers were not in vain. As St. Luke writes in his Gospel, "Nothing will be impossible for God" (1:37). God indeed worked many miracles for us. Once, while in the hospital, Stephen experienced sudden cardiac arrest during a shift change, meaning twice as many people were available to respond. Had there been fewer people, Stephen could easily have died. Not only did he survive, but he sustained no brain damage. The doctors were amazed.

Later, Stephen confided in me that he had an out-of-body experience during his cardiac arrest. A huge hand reached out to him and took him down a long tunnel with a bright light at the end. He felt no pain, but only such warmth and love that he didn't want to leave. But, he explained, a voice told him his time hadn't come. Then, he found himself back in his body.

"I'm not afraid of dying anymore," Stephen told me. "And when I die, I want to go to Heaven. I know that's where you'll be."

I couldn't contain my joy. Teetering on the edge between life and death, Stephen had finally accepted God's love. Once again, Our Lord had shown that our lives are in His hands. He had never walked away from Stephen — it was the other way around.

Stephen agreed to make his Confession to a priest friend of mine. He received Holy Communion and the apostolic blessing to prepare his soul for what lay ahead. These miracles alone would have been enough, but God continued to bless us abundantly.

After his cardiac arrest, Stephen relied on a newly devised machine to support his weak heart. Unexpectedly, while on the device, his heart began to beat in a life-threatening rhythm. This was a first! The cardiologists had never performed a cardioversion under these circumstances. Concerned and hard-pressed for answers, they held a conference call with a team of cardiology colleagues on the West Coast to determine how to proceed.

As we waited, Stephen told me with certainty that he was going to die. I comforted him and kept myself calm by praying one Hail Mary after another. I thought about what Stephen had told me after his cardiac arrest: "If I die, I am going to be okay, because I am now spiritually prepared to go to Heaven. And if I live, I will be okay, because I will have a new heart." In that moment of darkness, God had given us both the gift of faith.

"I'm going to call the nuns," I told Stephen.

Over the years, I had become friends with a group of cloistered nuns in our city. By now, they knew Stephen and me on a first-name basis. Their prayers had supported and consoled me throughout the trials of my marriage.

Sr. Mary answered the phone, and I shared my urgent prayer request. While the cardiologists were deliberating, I stepped outside and prayed with her. A few minutes after I hung up, one of the cardiologists approached me.

"Stephen converted spontaneously," he said, perplexed. "We didn't have to use the paddles or anything. It's a miracle."

Again, I rejoiced. God had given me friends with a direct line to Heaven!

Thanks to the wonderful doctors, nurses, and hospital staff, Stephen was the first patient in our state to survive a heart transplant. (Three others had undergone the procedure, but all had died.) Within a few weeks, he was able to come home from the hospital.

The next four months were wonderful: we took our first overseas trip to New Zealand and Australia with Friendship Force International, and we met the family of the heart donor whose selflessness had saved Stephen's life. When we placed a stethoscope on Stephen's chest for them to listen to his heartbeat, we all cried. God had blessed us so abundantly.

How was it that, after all these trials and graces, Stephen once again turned his back on the Faith? I still don't fully understand. He was a consummate con artist, very savvy and articulate, able to talk his way out of just about anything. Duplicity was a significant part of his new lease on life. He would arrange business trips and offer unimpeachable explanations for his absence. I knew he was hiding something, but without evidence, I couldn't pin him down.

With certainty and faith, I prayed that God would reveal the secrets Stephen was keeping from me. I asked Our Blessed Mother for her protection and intercession, and then I prepared my heart for the worst.

A few weeks later, I received an anonymous letter confirming my suspicions: Stephen was having an affair with his married law clerk. She was twenty-five years his junior and had young children.

I froze. I had no idea what to do.

"Lord, please help me," I prayed. "Send your Holy Spirit. Tell me what I should do."

I kept praying until Stephen returned home that evening. Unsurprisingly, he was prepared for our confrontation. The moment he walked in the door, he asked, "Did you get a letter today accusing me of having an affair?"

"You bet I did." I thrust the envelope at him.

"Yep, it looks just like the one Sarah's husband got," he said. There was his suave courtroom persona in high gear. "It did the trick. He's furious."

Then, he looked me in the eye and said, "You know it's not true, right? It's all just office politics, people trying to bring me and Sarah down."

By the grace of God, I did not back down. I shouted, "You want me to believe that? Come on! You're a liar, a cheater. It's an affront to our marriage vows, to me, and to your own reputation."

"You really think so? You know you can't believe everything you hear."

The room was spinning. I was sick to my stomach. I clenched my fists and was about to scream back at him when the Holy Spirit suddenly whispered to me. My anger wouldn't make Stephen tell the truth. He'd made his choice, and he would tell all the lies he needed to defend himself. All I could do was listen to God.

For days, I prayed as hard as I had when Stephen was on the brink of death. (God always knows how to get me down on my knees.) At work, I was on my best behavior and fought to stay cheerful. I couldn't confide in my coworkers or in my family. I didn't want the awful news to come back to haunt me. But I needed to confide in someone.

Then, the Holy Spirit came to me again. This time, He guided me to Our Blessed Mother and whispered, "Tell her all."

So I did: I confided to Mary all my thoughts, feelings, worries, concerns, and needs. In time, she guided me to a Catholic counselor. Without the counselor's support, Mary's intercession, and God's love, I could never have survived the pain Stephen caused me.

Things got worse: I found a love letter in Stephen's briefcase. In it, he told Sarah about his plan to leave me for her. (Never mind the two other women I found out he was seeing.) Even after Sarah quit her job at her husband's behest, she and Stephen continued their affair. I knew I had to get my finances in order so I wouldn't be left high and dry. I changed my will and continued to pray. God had guided me all my life; neither would He abandon me now, nor would He let Stephen continue to hide the truth from me.

Three months later, Stephen received more bad news from his doctors. The heart transplant had saved his life, but with a catch: his immune system had to be suppressed so that it would not reject the donor heart. Now he was facing a horrible consequence: pancreatic cancer. This time, we knew for sure he had received a death sentence.

The bottom seemed to fall out from under him. He tried to play on Sarah's sympathy. She couldn't possibly be there for him, but I was. As Stephen's helpmate, I resolved to assist him on the final steps of his journey toward eternity. I told him that I forgave him, not seven times, but seventy times seven. We talked about the severity of his cancer, the poor prognosis, and what lay ahead for both of us.

"You need to prepare to get your soul right with God," I said. "That's what we should pray for—spiritual healing, not physical healing."

The Holy Spirit and our guardian angels were with me as I tried to think of a priest who would be able to get through to Stephen. They led me to Fr. Ignatius, a newly ordained priest whom I had befriended and who seemed capable of going toe-to-toe with my husband.

Thank God for the sacrament of Reconciliation and for the priests who celebrate it. Fr. Ignatius was able to bring Stephen God's forgiveness, which so profoundly outweighs the heaviness of our sins. As Stephen himself told me (after some encouragement and gentle prodding), a burden had been lifted from his shoulders. In his last months, through the apostolic blessing, many prayers for divine mercy, and guidance for preparing his soul for eternity, he experienced comfort instead of fear; and when he closed his eyes for the last time, he was in a state of grace.

"The God of all grace who called you to his eternal glory through Christ [Jesus], will himself restore, confirm, strengthen, and establish you after you have suffered a little" (1 Pet. 5:10). How true these words are. Stephen had sinned greatly. He had strayed far from God, preferring to live on the edge, but Christ rescued him and called him to eternal glory.

After the High Mass for Stephen's funeral, during his burial service, the Holy Spirit gave me peace. In my heart, I knew Stephen was no longer conflicted. He was no longer running from God. After years and years, God answered my prayer. But he also fulfilled the silent longing Stephen must have felt in his soul. All the knowledge and thrills of the world couldn't quench his parched soul—only God could.

As St. Thomas Aquinas wrote in the *Summa Theologica*, "The more a thing is desired the more painful is its absence." I can't say for sure how much Stephen desired God or how much pain His absence caused. I know that I desired Stephen's salvation more than anything else, and so I suffered greatly while he strayed. Yet how much greater was my joy when he finally came home! To quote Aquinas again: "The soul suffers enormously from the delay," but when our suffering comes to an end, God truly fills us with unmatched joy.

About the Authors

Debbie Georgianni spent thirty years in catechetical ministry. She holds a graduate degree in theology and is a certified life and health coach, speaker, writer, and published author of a religious education curriculum. Debbie is co-host of EWTN Radio's popular weekday show *Take 2 with Jerry and Debbie*. The show was a recipient of a Gabriel Award in 2018.

Jerry Usher has spent more than forty years in broadcast media, including Catholic radio since 1996. He spent six years in formation for the priesthood from 1989 to 1995, receiving a bachelor's degree in philosophy and theology, and two years of master's studies in the seminary. Jerry is the co-editor of *Called by Name*, a collection of first-person testimonies about being called to the priesthood. He is co-host of EWTN Radio's *Take 2 with Jerry and Debbie*.

Jerry and Debbie have co-hosted *Take 2 with Jerry and Debbie* for the past five years. During that time, they have come to realize that the listeners and callers to the show have powerful life stories that can benefit us all—real-life experiences that provide wisdom that no class, program, or retreat can offer.